Using Asyncio in Python
Understanding Python's Asynchronous Programming Features

Caleb Hattingh

Beijing · Boston · Farnham · Sebastopol · Tokyo

Using Asyncio in Python

by Caleb Hattingh

Copyright © 2020 Tekmoji Pty Ltd. All rights reserved.

Published by O'Reilly Media, Inc., 1005 Gravenstein Highway North, Sebastopol, CA 95472.

O'Reilly books may be purchased for educational, business, or sales promotional use. Online editions are also available for most titles (*http://oreilly.com*). For more information, contact our corporate/institutional sales department: 800-998-9938 or *corporate@oreilly.com*.

Acquisitions Editor: Jessica Haberman
Developmental Editor: Corbin Collins
Production Editor: Beth Kelly
Copyeditor: Rachel Head
Proofreader: Sharon Wilkey

Indexer: Ellen Troutman-Zaig
Interior Designer: David Futato
Cover Designer: Karen Montgomery
Illustrator: Rebecca Demarest

February 2020:   First Edition

Revision History for the First Edition
2020-01-30:   First Release

See *http://oreilly.com/catalog/errata.csp?isbn=9781492075332* for release details.

978-1-492-07533-2

[LSI]

To my partner, Gina: I deeply appreciate all your encouragement and support while writing this book; it has made all the difference.

—Caleb

Table of Contents

Preface

Python 3.4 introduced the `asyncio` library, and Python 3.5 produced the `async` and `await` keywords to use it palatably. These new additions allow so-called *asynchronous* programming.

All of these new features, which I'll refer to under the single name *Asyncio*, have been received by the Python community somewhat warily; a segment of the community seems to see them as complex and difficult to understand. This view is not limited to beginners: several high-profile contributors to the Python community have expressed doubts about the complexity of the Asyncio API in Python, and educators in the community have expressed concern about how best to teach Asyncio to students.

Most people with a few years' experience with Python have used threads before, and even if you haven't, you are still likely to have experienced *blocking*. For example, if you've written programs using the wonderful `requests` library, you will surely have noticed that your program pauses for a bit while it does `requests.get(url)`; this is blocking behavior.

For one-off tasks, this is fine; but if you want to fetch *ten thousand* URLs simultaneously, it's going to be difficult to use `requests`. Large-scale concurrency is one big reason to learn and use Asyncio, but the other big attraction of Asyncio over preemptive threading is safety: it will be much easier for you to avoid race condition bugs with Asyncio.

My goal with this book is to give you a basic understanding of why these new features have been introduced and how to use them in your own projects. More specifically, I aim to provide the following:

- A critical comparison of `asyncio` and `threading` for concurrent network programming
- An understanding of the new `async`/`await` language syntax
- A general overview of the new `asyncio` standard library features in Python

- Detailed, extended case studies with code, showing how to use a few of the more popular Asyncio-compatible third-party libraries

We'll begin with a story that illustrates the shift in thinking that must accompany a transition from threaded to async programming. Then, we'll take a look at the changes that were made in the Python language itself to accommodate async programming. Finally, we'll explore some of the ways in which these new features can be used most effectively.

The new Asyncio features are not going to radically change the way you write programs. They provide specific tools that make sense only for specific situations; but in the right situations, `asyncio` is exceptionally useful. In this book, we're going to explore those situations and how you can best approach them by using the new Asyncio features.

Conventions Used in This Book

The following typographical conventions are used in this book:

Italic
    Indicates new terms, URLs, email addresses, filenames, and file extensions.

`Constant width`
    Used for program listings, as well as within paragraphs to refer to program elements such as variable or function names, databases, datatypes, environment variables, statements, and keywords.

`Constant width bold`
    Shows commands or other text that should be typed literally by the user.

`Constant width italic`
    Shows text that should be replaced with user-supplied values or by values determined by context.

This element signifies a tip or suggestion.

This element signifies a general note.

This element indicates a warning or caution.

O'Reilly Online Learning

 For more than 40 years, *O'Reilly Media* has provided technology and business training, knowledge, and insight to help companies succeed.

Our unique network of experts and innovators share their knowledge and expertise through books, articles, conferences, and our online learning platform. O'Reilly's online learning platform gives you on-demand access to live training courses, in-depth learning paths, interactive coding environments, and a vast collection of text and video from O'Reilly and 200+ other publishers. For more information, please visit *http://oreilly.com*.

How to Contact Us

Please address comments and questions concerning this book to the publisher:

O'Reilly Media, Inc.
1005 Gravenstein Highway North
Sebastopol, CA 95472
800-998-9938 (in the United States or Canada)
707-829-0515 (international or local)
707-829-0104 (fax)

We have a web page for this book, where we list errata, examples, and any additional information. It can be accessed at *https://oreil.ly/using-asyncio-in-python*.

Email *bookquestions@oreilly.com* to comment or ask technical questions about this book.

For more information about our books, courses, conferences, and news, see our website at *http://www.oreilly.com*.

Find us on Facebook: *http://facebook.com/oreilly*

Follow us on Twitter: *http://twitter.com/oreillymedia*

Watch us on YouTube: *http://www.youtube.com/oreillymedia*

Acknowledgments

Many thanks to Ashwini Balnaves and Kevin Baker for working through very early drafts of this book and providing invaluable feedback. I am deeply grateful to Yury Selivanov for making precious time available to review an earlier incarnation of this book, when it was first published as an O'Reilly report. Finally, I would also like to thank the team at O'Reilly for their excellent editorial support.

## CHAPTER 1

Introducing Asyncio

> My story is a lot like yours, only more interesting 'cause it involves robots.
>
> —Bender, *Futurama* episode "30% Iron Chef"

The most common question I receive about Asyncio in Python 3 is this: "What is it, and what do I do with it?" The answer you'll hear most frequently is likely something about being able to execute multiple concurrent HTTP requests in a single program. But there is more to it than that—much more. Asyncio requires changing how you think about structuring programs.

The following story provides a backdrop for gaining this understanding. The central focus of Asyncio is on how best to best perform multiple tasks at the same time—and not just any tasks, but specifically tasks that involve waiting periods. The key insight required with this style of programming is that while you wait for *this* task to complete, work on *other* tasks can be performed.

The Restaurant of ThreadBots

The year is 2051, and you find yourself in the restaurant business. Automation, largely by robot workers, powers most of the economy, but it turns out that humans still enjoy going out to eat once in a while. In your restaurant, all the employees are robots—humanoid, of course, but unmistakably robots. The most successful manufacturer of robots is Threading Inc., and robot workers from this company have come to be called "ThreadBots."

Except for this small robotic detail, your restaurant looks and operates like one of those old-time establishments from, say, 2020. Your guests will be looking for that vintage experience. They want fresh food prepared from scratch. They want to sit at tables. They want to wait for their meals—but only a little. They want to pay at the end, and they sometimes even want to leave a tip, for old times' sake.

Being new to the robotic restaurant business, you do what every other restaurateur does and hire a small fleet of robots: one to greet diners at the front desk (GreetBot), one to wait tables and take orders (WaitBot), one to do the cooking (ChefBot), and one to manage the bar (WineBot).

Hungry diners arrive at the front desk and are welcomed by GreetBot, your front-of-house ThreadBot. They are then directed to a table, and once they are seated, WaitBot takes their order. Then WaitBot brings that order to the kitchen on a slip of paper (because you want to preserve that old-time experience, remember?). ChefBot looks at the order on the slip and begins preparing the food. WaitBot will periodically check whether the food is ready, and when it is, will immediately take the dishes to the customers' table. When the guests are ready to leave, they return to GreetBot, who calculates the bill, takes their payment, and graciously wishes them a pleasant evening.

Your restaurant is a hit, and you soon grow to have a large customer base. Your robot employees do exactly what they're told, and they are perfectly good at the tasks you assign them. Everything is going really well, and you couldn't be happier.

Over time, however, you do begin to notice some problems. Oh, it's nothing truly serious; just a few things that seem to go wrong. Every other robotic restaurant owner seems to have similar niggling glitches. It is a little worrying that these problems seem to get worse the more successful you become.

Though rare, there are the occasional collisions that are very unsettling: sometimes, when a plate of food is ready in the kitchen, WaitBot will grab it *before* ChefBot has even let go of the plate. This usually ends up with the plate shattering and leaves a big mess. ChefBot cleans it up, of course, but still, you'd think that these top-notch robots would know how to be a bit more synchronized with each other. This happens at the bar too: sometimes WineBot will place a drink order on the bar, and WaitBot will grab it before WineBot has let go, resulting in broken glass and spilled Nederburg Cabernet Sauvignon.

Also, sometimes GreetBot will seat new diners at exactly the same moment that WaitBot has decided to clean what it thought was an empty table. It's pretty awkward for the diners. You've tried adding delay logic to WaitBot's cleaning function, or delays to GreetBot's seating function, but these don't really help, and the collisions still occur. But at least these events are rare.

Well, they used to be. Your restaurant has become so popular that you've had to hire a few more ThreadBots. For very busy Friday and Saturday evenings, you've had to add a second GreetBot and two extra WaitBots. Unfortunately, the hiring contracts for ThreadBots mean that you have to hire them for the whole week, so this effectively means that for most of the quiet part of the week, you're carrying three extra ThreadBots that you don't really need.

The other resource problem, in addition to the extra cost, is that it's more work for you to deal with these extra ThreadBots. It was fine to keep tabs on just four bots, but now you're up to seven. Keeping track of seven ThreadBots is a lot more work, and because your restaurant keeps getting more and more famous, you become worried about taking on even more ThreadBots. It's going to become a full-time job just to keep track of what each ThreadBot is doing. And another thing: these extra Thread-Bots are using up a lot more space inside your restaurant. It's becoming a tight squeeze for your customers, what with all these robots zipping around. You're worried that if you need to add even more bots, this space problem is going to get even worse. You want to use the space in your restaurant for customers, not ThreadBots.

The collisions have also become worse since you added more ThreadBots. Now, sometimes two WaitBots take the exact same order from the same table at the same time. It's as if they both noticed that the table was ready to order and moved in to take it, without noticing that the other WaitBot was doing the exact same thing. As you can imagine, this results in duplicated food orders, which causes extra load on the kitchen and increases the chance of collisions when picking up the ready plates. You're concerned that if you add more WaitBots, this problem might get worse.

Time passes.

Then, during one very, very busy Friday night service, you have a singular moment of clarity: time slows, lucidity overwhelms you, and you see a snapshot of your restaurant frozen in time. *My ThreadBots are doing nothing!* Not really nothing, to be fair, but they're just…waiting.

Each of your three WaitBots at different tables is waiting for one of the diners at their table to give their order. The WineBot has already prepared 17 drinks, which are now waiting to be collected (it took only a few seconds), and is waiting for a new drink order. One of the GreetBots has greeted a new party of guests and told them they need to wait a minute to be seated, and is waiting for the guests to respond. The other GreetBot, now processing a credit card payment for another guest that is leaving, is waiting for confirmation on the payment gateway device. Even the ChefBot, who is currently cooking 35 meals, is not actually doing anything at this moment, but is simply waiting for one of the meals to complete cooking so that it can be plated up and handed over to a WaitBot.

You realize that even though your restaurant is now full of ThreadBots, and you're even considering getting more (with all the problems that entails), the ones that you currently have are not being fully utilized.

The moment passes, but not the realization. On Sunday, you add a data collection module to your ThreadBots. For each ThreadBot, you're measuring how much time is spent waiting and how much is spent actively doing work. Over the course of the following week, the data is collected. Then on Sunday evening, you analyze the results. It turns out that even when your restaurant is at full capacity, the most hard-working ThreadBot is idle about 98% of the time. The ThreadBots are so enormously efficient that they can perform any task in fractions of a second.

As an entrepreneur, this inefficiency really bugs you. You know that every other robotic restaurant owner is running their business the same as you, with many of the same problems. But, you think, slamming your fist on your desk, "There must be a better way!"

So the very next day, which is a quiet Monday, you try something bold: you program a single ThreadBot to do all the tasks. Every time it begins to wait, even for a second, the ThreadBot switches to the next task to be done in the restaurant, whatever it may be, instead of waiting. It sounds incredible—only one ThreadBot doing the work of all the others—but you're confident that your calculations are correct. And besides, Monday is a quiet day; even if something goes wrong, the impact will be small. For this new project, you call the bot "LoopBot" because it will loop over all the jobs in the restaurant.

The programming was more difficult than usual. It isn't just that you had to program one ThreadBot with all the different tasks; you also had to program some of the logic of when to switch between tasks. But by this stage, you've had a lot of experience with programming these ThreadBots, so you manage to get it done.

You watch your LoopBot like a hawk. It moves between stations in fractions of a second, checking whether there is work to be done. Not long after opening, the first guest arrives at the front desk. The LoopBot shows up almost immediately, and asks whether the guest would like a table near the window or near the bar. But then, as the LoopBot begins to wait, its programming tells it to switch to the next task, and it whizzes off. This seems like a dreadful error, but then you see that as the guest begins to say "Window please," the LoopBot is back. It receives the answer and directs the guest to table 42. And off it goes again, checking for drink orders, food orders, table cleanup, and arriving guests, over and over again.

Late Monday evening, you congratulate yourself on a remarkable success. You check the data collection module on the LoopBot, and it confirms that even with a single ThreadBot doing the work of seven, the idle time was still around 97%. This result gives you the confidence to continue the experiment all through the rest of the week.

As the busy Friday service approaches, you reflect on the great success of your experiment. For service during a normal working week, you can easily manage the workload with a single LoopBot. And you've noticed another thing: you don't see any more collisions. This makes sense; since there is only one LoopBot, it cannot get confused with itself. No more duplicate orders going to the kitchen, and no more confusion about when to grab a plate or drink.

Friday evening service begins, and as you had hoped, the single ThreadBot keeps up with all the customers and tasks, and service is proceeding even better than before. You imagine that you can take on even more customers now, and you don't have to worry about having to bring on more ThreadBots. You think of all the money you're going to save.

Then, unfortunately, something goes wrong: one of the meals, an intricate soufflé, has flopped. This has never happened before in your restaurant. You begin to study the LoopBot more closely. It turns out that at one of your tables, there is a very chatty guest. This guest has come to your restaurant alone and keeps trying to make conversation with the LoopBot, even sometimes holding your LoopBot by the hand. When this happens, your LoopBot is unable to dash off and attend to the ever-growing list of tasks elsewhere in your restaurant. This is why the kitchen produced its first flopped soufflé: your LoopBot was unable to make it back to the kitchen to remove the dish from the oven because it was held up by a guest.

Friday service finishes, and you head home to reflect on what you have learned. It's true that the LoopBot was able to do all the work that was required in the busy Friday service; but on the other hand, your kitchen produced its very first spoiled meal, something that has never happened before. Chatty guests used to keep WaitBots busy all the time, but that never affected the kitchen service at all.

All things considered, you decide it is still better to continue using a single LoopBot. Those worrying collisions no longer occur, and there is much more space in your restaurant—space that you can use for more customers. But you realize something profound about the LoopBot: it can be effective only if every task is short, or at least can be performed in a short period of time. If any activity keeps the LoopBot busy for too long, other tasks will begin to suffer neglect.

It is difficult to know in advance which tasks may take too much time. What if a guest orders a cocktail that requires intricate preparation, taking much more time than usual? What if a guest wants to complain about a meal at the front desk, refuses to pay, and grabs the LoopBot by the arm, preventing it from task switching? You decide that instead of figuring out all of these issues up front, it is better to continue with the LoopBot, record as much information as possible, and deal with any problems later as they arise.

More time passes.

Gradually, other restaurant owners notice your operation, and eventually they figure out that they too can get by, and even thrive, with only a single ThreadBot. Word spreads. Soon every single restaurant operates in this way, and it becomes difficult to remember that robotic restaurants ever operated with multiple ThreadBots at all.

Epilogue

In our story, each robot worker in the restaurant is a single thread. The key observation in the story is that the nature of the work in the restaurant involves a great deal of waiting, just as `requests.get()` is waiting for a response from a server.

In a restaurant, the worker time spent waiting isn't huge when slow humans are doing manual work, but when super-efficient and quick robots are doing the work, nearly all their time is spent waiting. In computer programming, the same is true when network programming is involved. CPUs do work and wait on network I/O. CPUs in modern computers are extremely fast—hundreds of thousands of times faster than network traffic. Thus, CPUs running networking programs spend a great deal of time waiting.

The insight in the story is that programs can be written to explicitly direct the CPU to move between work tasks as necessary. Although there is an improvement in economy (using fewer CPUs for the same work), the real advantage, compared to a threading (multi-CPU) approach, is the elimination of race conditions.

It's not all roses, however: as we found in the story, there are benefits and drawbacks to most technology solutions. The introduction of the LoopBot solved a certain class of problems but also introduced new problems—not the least of which is that the restaurant owner had to learn a slightly different way of programming.

What Problem Is Asyncio Trying to Solve?

For I/O-bound workloads, there are exactly (only!) two reasons to use async-based concurrency over thread-based concurrency:

- Asyncio offers a safer alternative to preemptive multitasking (i.e., using threads), thereby avoiding the bugs, race conditions, and other nondeterministic dangers that frequently occur in nontrivial threaded applications.

- Asyncio offers a simple way to support many thousands of *simultaneous* socket connections, including being able to handle many long-lived connections for newer technologies like WebSockets, or MQTT for Internet of Things (IoT) applications.

That's it.

Threading—as a programming model—is best suited to certain kinds of computational tasks that are best executed with multiple CPUs and shared memory for efficient communication between the threads. In such tasks, the use of multicore processing with shared memory is a necessary evil because the problem domain requires it.

Network programming is *not* one of those domains. The key insight is that network programming involves a great deal of "waiting for things to happen," and because of this, we don't need the operating system to efficiently distribute our tasks over multiple CPUs. Furthermore, we don't need the risks that preemptive multitasking brings, such as race conditions when working with shared memory.

However, there is a great deal of misinformation about other supposed benefits of event-based programming models. Here are a few of the things that just ain't so:

Asyncio will make my code blazing fast.
> Unfortunately, no. In fact, most benchmarks seem to show that threading solutions are slightly faster than their comparable Asyncio solutions. If the extent of concurrency itself is considered a performance metric, Asyncio *does* make it a bit easier to create very large numbers of concurrent socket connections, though. Operating systems often have limits on how many threads can be created, and this number is significantly lower than the number of socket connections that can be made. The OS limits can be changed, but it is certainly easier to do with Asyncio. And while we expect that having many thousands of threads should incur extra *context-switching* costs that coroutines avoid, it turns out to be difficult to benchmark this in practice.[1] No, speed is not the benefit of Asyncio in Python; if that's what you're after, try *Cython* instead!

Asyncio makes threading redundant.
> Definitely not! The true value of threading lies in being able to write multi-CPU programs, in which different computational tasks can share memory. The numerical library numpy, for instance, already makes use of this by speeding up certain matrix calculations through the use of multiple CPUs, even though all the memory is shared. For sheer performance, there is no competitor to this programming model for CPU-bound computation.

Asyncio removes the problems with the GIL.
> Again, no. It is true that Asyncio is not *affected* by the GIL,[2] but this is only because the GIL affects multithreaded programs. The "problems" with the GIL that people refer to occur because it prevents true multicore parallelism when using threads. Since Asyncio is single-threaded (almost by definition), it is unaffected by the GIL, but it cannot benefit from multiple CPU cores either.[3] It is also

---

1 Research in this area seems hard to find, but the numbers seem to be around 50 microseconds per threaded context switch on Linux on modern hardware. To give a (very) rough idea: one thousand threads implies 50 ms total cost just for the context switching. It does add up, but it isn't going to wreck your application either.

2 The *global interpreter lock* (GIL) makes the Python interpreter code (not *your* code!) thread-safe by locking the processing of each opcode; it has the unfortunate side effect of effectively pinning the execution of the interpreter to a single CPU, and thus preventing multicore parallelism.

3 This is similar to why JavaScript lacks a GIL "problem": there is only one thread.

worth pointing out that in multithreaded code, the Python GIL can cause additional performance problems beyond what has already been mentioned in other points: Dave Beazley presented a talk on this called "Understanding the Python GIL" (*https://oreil.ly/n_D3N*) at PyCon 2010, and much of what is discussed in that talk remains true today.

Asyncio prevents all race conditions.
False. The possibility of race conditions is always present with any concurrent programming, regardless of whether threading or event-based programming is used. It is true that Asyncio can virtually eliminate a certain *class* of race conditions common in multithreaded programs, such as intra-process shared memory access. However, it doesn't eliminate the possibility of other kinds of race conditions, such as the interprocess races with shared resources common in distributed microservices architectures. You must still pay attention to how shared resources are being used. The main advantage of Asyncio over threaded code is that the points at which control of execution is transferred between coroutines are *visible* (because of the presence of `await` keywords), and thus it is much easier to reason about how shared resources are being accessed.

Asyncio makes concurrent programming easy.
Ahem, where do I even begin?

The last myth is the most dangerous one. Dealing with concurrency is *always* complex, regardless of whether you're using threading or Asyncio. When experts say "Asyncio makes concurrency easier," what they really mean is that Asyncio makes it a little easier to avoid certain kinds of truly nightmarish race condition bugs—the kind that keep you up at night and that you tell other programmers about in hushed tones over campfires, wolves howling in the distance.

Even with Asyncio, there is still a great deal of complexity to deal with. How will your application support health checks? How will you communicate with a database that may allow only a few connections—much fewer than your five thousand socket connections to clients? How will your program terminate connections gracefully when you receive a signal to shut down? How will you handle (blocking!) disk access and logging? These are just a few of the many complex design decisions that you will have to answer.

Application design will still be difficult, but the hope is that you will have an easier time reasoning about your application logic when you have only one thread to deal with.

## CHAPTER 2

The Truth About Threads

Let's be frank for a moment—you really don't want to use Curio. All things equal, you should probably be programming with threads. Yes, threads. THOSE threads. Seriously. I'm not kidding.

—Dave Beazley, "Developing with Curio" (*https://oreil.ly/oXJaC*)

If you've never heard of threads before, here's a basic description: threads are a feature provided by an operating system (OS), made available to software developers so that they may indicate to the OS which parts of their program may be run in parallel. The OS decides how to share CPU resources with each of the parts, much as the OS decides to share CPU resources with all the other different programs (processes) running at the same time.

Since you're reading an Asyncio book, this must be the part where I tell you, "Threads are terrible, and you should never use them," right? Unfortunately, the situation is not so simple. We need to weigh the benefits and risks of using threads, just like with any technology choice.

This book is not supposed to be about threads at all. But there are two problems here: Asyncio is offered as an alternative to threading, so it's hard to understand the value proposition without some comparison; and even when using Asyncio, you will still likely have to deal with threads and processes, so you need to know something about threading.

 The context of this discussion is exclusively concurrency in network programming applications. Preemptive multithreading is also used in other domains, where the trade-offs are entirely different.

Benefits of Threading

These are the main benefits of threading:

Ease of reading code
> Your code can run concurrently, but still be set out in a very simple, top-down linear sequence of commands to the point where—and this is key—you can pretend, within the body of your functions, that no concurrency is happening.

Parallelism with shared memory
> Your code can exploit multiple CPUs while still having threads share memory. This is important in many workloads where it would be too costly to move large amounts of data between the separate memory spaces of different processes, for example.

Know-how and existing code
> There is a large body of knowledge and best practices available for writing threaded applications. There is also a huge amount of existing "blocking" code that depends on multithreading for concurrent operation.

Now, with *Python*, the point about parallelism is questionable because the Python interpreter uses a global lock, called the *global interpreter lock* (GIL), to protect the internal state of the interpreter itself. That is, it provides protection from the potential catastrophic effects of race conditions between multiple threads. A side effect of the lock is that it ends up pinning all threads in your program to a single CPU. As you might imagine, this negates any parallelism performance benefits (unless you use tools like Cython or Numba to maneuver around the limitation).

The first point regarding perceived simplicity, however, is significant: threading in Python *feels* exceptionally simple, and if you haven't been burned before by impossibly hard race condition bugs, threading offers a very attractive concurrency model. Even if you have been burned in the past, threading remains a compelling option because you will likely have learned (the hard way) how to keep your code both simple and safe.

I don't have space to get into safer threaded programming here, but generally speaking, the best practice for using threads is to use the `ThreadPoolExecutor` class from the `concurrent.futures` module, passing all required data in through the `submit()` method. Example 2-1 shows a basic example.

Example 2-1. Best practice for threading

```
from concurrent.futures import ThreadPoolExecutor as Executor

def worker(data):
    <process the data>
```

```
with Executor(max_workers=10) as exe:
    future = exe.submit(worker, data)
```

The `ThreadPoolExecutor` offers an extremely simple interface for running functions in a thread—and the best part is that, if needed, you can convert the pool of threads into a pool of subprocesses simply by using `ProcessPoolExecutor` instead. It has the same API as `ThreadPoolExecutor`, which means that your code will be little affected by the change. The executor API is also used in `asyncio` and is described in the next chapter (see Example 3-3).

In general, you'll prefer your tasks to be somewhat short-lived, so that when your program needs to shut down, you can simply call `Executor.shutdown(wait=True)` and wait a second or two to allow the executor to complete.

Most importantly: if at all possible, you should try to prevent your threaded code (in the preceding example, the `worker()` function) from accessing or writing to any global variables!

 Raymond Hettinger presented several great guidelines for safer threaded code at PyCon Russia 2016 (*https://oreil.ly/ZZVps*) and PyBay 2017 (*https://oreil.ly/JDplJ*). I strongly urge you to add these videos to your watch list.

Drawbacks of Threading

[N]ontrivial multithreaded programs are incomprehensible to humans. It is true that the programming model can be improved through the use of design patterns, better granularity of atomicity (e.g., transactions), improved languages, and formal methods. However, these techniques merely chip away at the unnecessarily enormous non-determinism of the threading model. The model remains intrinsically intractable.

—Edward A. Lee "The Problem with Threads" (*http://bit.ly/2CFOv8a*)

The drawbacks of threading have been mentioned in a few other places already, but for completeness let's collect them here anyway:

Threading is difficult
Threading bugs and race conditions in threaded programs are *the hardest* kinds of bugs to fix. With experience, it is possible to design new software that is less prone to these problems, but in nontrivial, naively designed software, they can be nearly impossible to fix, even by experts. Really!

Threads are resource-intensive
Threads require extra operating system resources to create, such as preallocated, per-thread stack space that consumes process virtual memory up front. This is a big problem with 32-bit operating systems, because the address space per process

is limited to 3 GB.[1] Nowadays, with the widespread availability of 64-bit operating systems, virtual memory isn't as precious as it used to be (addressable space for virtual memory is typically 48 bits; i.e., 256 TiB). On modern desktop operating systems, the physical memory required for stack space for each thread isn't even allocated by the OS until it is required, including stack space per thread. For example, on a modern, 64-bit Fedora 29 Linux with 8 GB memory, creating 10,000 do-nothing threads with this short snippet:

```
# threadmem.py
import os
from time import sleep
from threading import Thread
threads = [
  Thread(target=lambda: sleep(60)) for i in range(10000)
]
[t.start() for t in threads]
print(f'PID = {os.getpid()}')
[t.join() for t in threads]
```

leads to the following information in top:

```
MiB Mem : 7858.199 total, 1063.844 free, 4900.477 used
MiB Swap: 7935.996 total, 4780.934 free, 3155.062 used

   PID USER     PR  NI    VIRT    RES    SHR COMMAND
 15166 caleb    20   0 80.291g 131.1m   4.8m python3
```

Preallocated virtual memory is a staggering ~80 GB (due to 8 MB stack space per thread!), but resident memory is only ~130 MB. On a 32-bit Linux system, I would be unable to create this many because of the 3 GB user-space address-space limit, *regardless* of actual consumption of physical memory. To get around this problem on 32-bit systems, it is sometimes necessary to decrease the preconfigured stack size, which you can still do in Python today, with `threading.stack_size([size])`. Obviously, decreasing stack size has implications for runtime safety with respect to the degree to which function calls may be nested, including recursion. Single-threaded coroutines have none of these problems and are a far superior alternative for concurrent I/O.

Threading can affect throughput
At very high concurrency levels (say, >5,000 threads), there can also be an impact on throughput due to context-switching (*https://oreil.ly/eFQKQ*) costs, assuming you can figure out how to configure your operating system to even allow you to

---

1 The theoretical address space for a 32-bit process is 4 GB, but the operating system typically reserves some of that. Often, only 3 GB is left to the process as addressable virtual memory, but on some operating systems it can be as low as 2 GB. Please take the numbers mentioned in this section as generalizations and not absolutes. There are far too many platform-specific (and historically sensitive) details to get into here.

create that many threads! It has become so tedious on recent macOS versions, for example, to test the preceding 10,000 do-nothing-threads example, that I gave up trying to raise the limits at all.

Threading is inflexible

The operating system will continually share CPU time with all threads regardless of whether a thread is ready to do work or not. For instance, a thread may be waiting for data on a socket, but the OS scheduler may still switch to and from that thread thousands of times before any actual work needs to be done. (In the async world, the `select()` system call is used to check whether a socket-awaiting coroutine needs a turn; if not, that coroutine isn't even woken up, avoiding any switching costs completely.)

None of this information is new, and the problems with threading as a programming model are not platform-specific either. For example, this is what the Microsoft Visual C++ documentation (*http://bit.ly/2Fr3eXK*) says about threading:

> The central concurrency mechanism in the Windows API is the thread. You typically use the CreateThread function to create threads. Although threads are relatively easy to create and use, the operating system allocates a significant amount of time and other resources to manage them. Additionally, although each thread is guaranteed to receive the same execution time as any other thread at the same priority level, the associated overhead requires that you create sufficiently large tasks. For smaller or more fine-grained tasks, the overhead that is associated with concurrency can outweigh the benefit of running the tasks in parallel.

But—I hear you protest—this is *Windows*, right? Surely a Unix system doesn't have these problems? Here follows a similar recommendation from the Mac Developer Library's Threading Programming Guide (*https://oreil.ly/W3mBM*):

> Threading has a real cost to your program (and the system) in terms of memory use and performance. Each thread requires the allocation of memory in both the kernel memory space and your program's memory space. The core structures needed to manage your thread and coordinate its scheduling are stored in the kernel using wired memory. Your thread's stack space and per-thread data is stored in your program's memory space. Most of these structures are created and initialized when you first create the thread—a process that can be relatively expensive because of the required interactions with the kernel.

They go even further in the Concurrency Programming Guide (*https://oreil.ly/fcGNL*) (emphasis mine):

> In the past, introducing concurrency to an application required the creation of one or more additional threads. Unfortunately, writing threaded code is challenging. Threads are a low-level tool that must be managed manually. Given that the optimal number of threads for an application can change dynamically based on the current system load and the underlying hardware, implementing a correct threading solution becomes *extremely difficult*, if not impossible to achieve. In addition, the synchronization

mechanisms typically used with threads add complexity and risk to software designs without any guarantees of improved performance.

These themes repeat throughout:

- Threading makes code hard to reason about.
- Threading is an inefficient model for large-scale concurrency (thousands of concurrent tasks).

Next, let's look at a case study involving threads that highlights the first and most important point.

Case Study: Robots and Cutlery

> Second, and more important, we did not (and still do not) believe in the standard multithreading model, which is preemptive concurrency with shared memory: we still think that no one can write correct programs in a language where "a = a + 1" is not deterministic.
>
> —Roberto Ierusalimschy et al., "The Evolution of Lua" (*http://bit.ly/2Fq9M8P*)

At the start of this book, I told the story of a restaurant in which humanoid robots— ThreadBots—did all the work. In that analogy, each worker was a thread. In the case study in Example 2-2, we're going to look at *why* threading is considered unsafe.

Example 2-2. ThreadBot programming for table service

```python
import threading
from queue import Queue

class ThreadBot(threading.Thread):      ❶
    def __init__(self):
        super().__init__(target=self.manage_table)      ❷
        self.cutlery = Cutlery(knives=0, forks=0)      ❸
        self.tasks = Queue()      ❹

    def manage_table(self):
        while True:      ❺
            task = self.tasks.get()
            if task == 'prepare table':
                kitchen.give(to=self.cutlery, knives=4, forks=4)      ❻
            elif task == 'clear table':
                self.cutlery.give(to=kitchen, knives=4, forks=4)
            elif task == 'shutdown':
                return
```

❶ A ThreadBot is a subclass of a thread.

❷ The target function of the thread is the `manage_table()` method, defined later in the file.

❸ This bot is going to be waiting tables and will need to be responsible for some cutlery. Each bot keeps track of the cutlery that it took from the kitchen here. (The `Cutlery` class will be defined later.)

❹ The bot will also be assigned tasks. They will be added to this task queue, and the bot will perform them during its main processing loop, next.

❺ The primary routine of this bot is this infinite loop. If you need to shut down a bot, you have to give them the `shutdown` task.

❻ There are only three tasks defined for this bot. This one, `prepare table`, is what the bot must do to get a new table ready for service. For our test, the only requirement is to get sets of cutlery from the kitchen and place them on the table. `clear table` is used when a table is to be cleared: the bot must return the used cutlery back to the kitchen. `shutdown` just shuts down the bot.

Example 2-3 shows the definition of the `Cutlery` object.

Example 2-3. Definition of the Cutlery object

```
from attr import attrs, attrib

@attrs    ❶
class Cutlery:
    knives = attrib(default=0)    ❷
    forks = attrib(default=0)

    def give(self, to: 'Cutlery', knives=0, forks=0):    ❸
        self.change(-knives, -forks)
        to.change(knives, forks)

    def change(self, knives, forks):    ❹
            self.knives += knives
            self.forks += forks

kitchen = Cutlery(knives=100, forks=100)    ❺
bots = [ThreadBot() for i in range(10)]    ❻

import sys
for bot in bots:
    for i in range(int(sys.argv[1])):    ❼
        bot.tasks.put('prepare table')
        bot.tasks.put('clear table')
    bot.tasks.put('shutdown')    ❽
```

```
print('Kitchen inventory before service:', kitchen)
for bot in bots:
    bot.start()

for bot in bots:
    bot.join()
print('Kitchen inventory after service:', kitchen)
```

❶ attrs, which is an open source Python library that has nothing to do with threads or asyncio, is a really wonderful library for making class creation easy. Here, the @attrs decorator will ensure that this Cutlery class will get all the usual boilerplate code (like __init__()) automatically set up.

❷ The attrib() function provides an easy way to create attributes, including defaults, which you might normally have handled as keyword arguments in the __init__() method.

❸ This method is used to transfer knives and forks from one Cutlery object to another. Typically, it will be used by bots to obtain cutlery from the kitchen for new tables, and to return the cutlery back to the kitchen after a table is cleared.

❹ This is a very simple utility function for altering the inventory data in the object instance.

❺ We've defined kitchen as the identifier for the kitchen inventory of cutlery. Typically, each of the bots will obtain cutlery from this location. It is also required that they return cutlery to this store when a table is cleared.

❻ This script is executed when testing. For our test, we'll be using 10 ThreadBots.

❼ We get the number of tables as a command-line parameter, and then give each bot that number of tasks for preparing and clearing tables in the restaurant.

❽ The shutdown task will make the bots stop (so that bot.join() a bit further down will return). The rest of the script prints diagnostic messages and starts up the bots.

Your strategy for testing the code basically involves running a group of ThreadBots over a sequence of table service. Each ThreadBot must do the following:

- *Prepare* a "table for four," which means obtaining four sets of knives and forks from the kitchen.

- *Clear* a table, which means returning the set of four knives and forks from a table back to the kitchen.

If you run a bunch of ThreadBots over a bunch of tables a specific number of times, you expect that after all the work is done, all of the knives and forks should be back in the kitchen and accounted for.

Wisely, you decide to test that, with one hundred tables to be prepared and cleared by each ThreadBot and all of them operating at the same time, because you want to ensure that they can work together and nothing goes wrong. This is the output of that test:

```
$ python cutlery_test.py 100
Kitchen inventory before service: Cutlery(knives=100, forks=100)
Kitchen inventory after service: Cutlery(knives=100, forks=100)
```

All the knives and forks end up back in the kitchen! So, you congratulate yourself on writing good code and deploy the bots. Unfortunately, *in practice*, every now and then you find that you *do not* end up with all cutlery accounted for when the restaurant closes. You notice the problem gets worse when you add more bots and/or the place gets busier. Frustrated, you run your tests again, changing nothing except the size of the test (10,000 tables!):

```
$ python cutlery_test.py 10000
Kitchen inventory before service: Cutlery(knives=100, forks=100)
Kitchen inventory after service: Cutlery(knives=96, forks=108)
```

Oops. Now you see that there is indeed a problem. With 10,000 tables served, you end up with the wrong number of knives and forks left in the kitchen. For reproducibility, you check that the error is consistent:

```
$ python cutlery_test.py 10000
Kitchen inventory before service: Cutlery(knives=100, forks=100)
Kitchen inventory after service: Cutlery(knives=112, forks=96)
```

There are still errors, but *by different amounts* compared to the previous run. That's just ridiculous! Remember, these bots are exceptionally well constructed and they don't make mistakes. What could be going wrong?

Let's summarize the situation:

- Your ThreadBot code is very simple and easy to read. The logic is fine.
- You have a working test (with 100 tables) that reproducibly passes.
- You have a longer test (with 10,000 tables) that reproducibly fails.
- The longer test fails in *different, nonreproducible ways.*

These are a few typical signs of a race condition bug. Experienced readers will already have seen the cause, so let's investigate that now. It all comes down to this method inside our `Cutlery` class:

```
def change(self, knives, forks):
    self.knives += knives
    self.forks += forks
```

The inline summation, `+=`, is implemented internally (inside the C code for the Python interpreter itself) as a few separate steps:

1. Read the current value, `self.knives`, into a temporary location.

2. Add the new value, `knives`, to the value in that temporary location.

3. Copy the new total from the temporary location back into the original location.

The problem with preemptive multitasking is that any thread busy with these steps can be interrupted *at any time*, and a different thread can be given the opportunity to work through the same steps.

In this case, suppose ThreadBot *A* does step 1, and then the OS scheduler pauses *A* and switches to ThreadBot *B*. *B also* reads the current value of `self.knives`; then execution goes back to *A*. *A* increments its total and writes it back—but then *B* continues from where it got paused (after step 1), and it increments and writes back *its* new total, thereby *erasing* the change made by *A*!

 While this may sound complex, this example of a race condition is just about the simplest possible case. We were able to check *all* the code, and we even have tests that can reproduce the problem on demand. In the real world, in large projects, try to imagine how much more difficult it can become!

This problem can be fixed by placing a *lock* around the modification of the shared state (imagine we added a `threading.Lock` to the `Cutlery` class):

```
def change(self, knives, forks):
    with self.lock:
        self.knives += knives
        self.forks += forks
```

But this requires you to know all the places where state will be shared between multiple threads. This approach is viable when you control all the source code, but it becomes very difficult when many third-party libraries are used—which is likely in Python thanks to the wonderful open source ecosystem.

Note that it was not possible to see the race condition by looking at the source code alone. This is because the source code provides no hints about where execution is going to switch between threads. That wouldn't be useful anyway, because the OS can switch between threads just about anywhere.

Another, much better, solution—and the point of async programming—is to modify our code so that we use only one ThreadBot and configure it to move between *all* the tables as necessary. For our case study, this means that the knives and forks in the kitchen will get modified by only a single thread.

And even better, in our async programs, we'll be able to see exactly where context will switch between multiple concurrent coroutines, because the `await` keyword indicates such places explicitly. I've decided against showing an async version of this case study here, because Chapter 3 explains how to use `asyncio` in depth. But if your curiosity is insatiable, there is an annotated example in Example B-1; it'll probably only make sense after you read the next chapter!

Asyncio Walk-Through

> Asyncio provides another tool for concurrent programming in Python, that is more lightweight than threads or multiprocessing. In a very simple sense it does this by having an event loop execute a collection of tasks, with a key difference being that each task chooses when to yield control back to the event loop.
>
> —Philip Jones, "Understanding Asyncio" (*http://bit.ly/2EPys9Q*)

The `asyncio` API in Python is complex because it aims to solve different problems for different groups of people. Unfortunately, very little guidance is available to help you figure out which parts of `asyncio` are important for the group *you're* in.

My goal is to help you figure that out. There are two main target audiences for the async features in Python:

End-user developers

These want to make applications using `asyncio`. I am going to assume that you're in this group.

Framework developers

These want to make frameworks and libraries that end-user developers can use in their applications.

Much of the confusion around `asyncio` in the community today is due to lack of understanding of this difference. For instance, the official Python documentation for `asyncio` is more appropriate for framework developers than end users. This means that end-user developers reading those docs quickly become shell-shocked by the apparent complexity. You're somewhat forced to take it all in before being able to do anything with it.

It is my hope that this book can help you distinguish between the features of Asyncio that are important for end-user developers and those important for framework developers.

 If you're interested in the lower-level details around how concurrency frameworks like Asyncio are built internally, I highly recommend a wonderful talk by Dave Beazley, "Python Concurrency from the Ground Up: LIVE!" (*https://oreil.ly/_68Rm*), in which he demonstrates putting together a simpler version of an async framework like Asyncio.

My goal is to give you only the most basic understanding of the building blocks of Asyncio—enough that you should be able to write simple programs with it, and certainly enough that you will be able to dive into more complete references.[1]

First up, we have a "quickstart" section that introduces the most important building blocks for Asyncio applications.

Quickstart

> You only need to know about seven functions to use Asyncio [for everyday use].
>
> —Yury Selivanov, author of PEP 492, which added the async and await keywords to Python

It's pretty scary diving into the official documentation (*https://oreil.ly/4Y_Pd*) for Asyncio. There are many sections with new, enigmatic words and concepts that will be unfamiliar to even experienced Python programmers, as Asyncio is a very new thing in Python. I'm going to break all that down and explain how to approach the asyncio module documentation later, but for now you need to know that the actual surface area you have to worry about with the asyncio library is much smaller than it seems.

Yury Selivanov, the author of PEP 492 (*https://oreil.ly/I3K7H*) and all-round major contributor to async Python, explained in his PyCon 2016 talk "async/await in Python 3.5 and Why It Is Awesome," (*https://oreil.ly/ImGca*) that many of the APIs in the asyncio module are really intended for framework designers, not end-user developers. In that talk, he emphasized the main features that end users should care about. These are a small subset of the whole asyncio API and can be summarized as follows:

---

1 When they become available! At the time of writing, the only available references for Asyncio were the API specification in the official Python documentation and a collection of blog posts, several of which have been linked to in this book.

- Starting the `asyncio` event loop
- Calling `async/await` functions
- Creating a *task* to be run on the loop
- Waiting for multiple tasks to complete
- Closing the loop after all concurrent tasks have completed

In this section, we're going to look at those core features and see how to hit the ground looping with event-based programming in Python.

The "Hello World" of Asyncio in Python looks like Example 3-1.

Example 3-1. The "Hello World" of Asyncio

```
# quickstart.py
import asyncio, time

async def main():
    print(f'{time.ctime()} Hello!')
    await asyncio.sleep(1.0)
    print(f'{time.ctime()} Goodbye!')

asyncio.run(main())   ❶
```

❶ asyncio provides a `run()` function to execute an `async def` function and all other coroutines called from there, like `sleep()` in the `main()` function.

Here's the output from running Example 3-1:

```
$ python quickstart.py
Sun Aug 18 02:14:34 2019 Hello!
Sun Aug 18 02:14:35 2019 Goodbye!
```

In practice, most of your Asyncio-based code will use the `run()` function shown here, but it's important to understand a little more about what that function is doing for you. This understanding is important because it will influence how you design larger applications.

Example 3-2 is what I'll call a "Hello-ish World" example. It isn't exactly the same as what `run()` does, but it's close enough to introduce the ideas that we'll build on throughout the rest of the book. You'll need a basic knowledge of coroutines (discussed in depth later in this chapter), but try to follow along anyway and focus on the high-level concepts for now.

Example 3-2. The "Hello-ish World" of Asyncio

```python
# quickstart.py
import asyncio
import time

async def main():
    print(f"{time.ctime()} Hello!")
    await asyncio.sleep(1.0)
    print(f"{time.ctime()} Goodbye!")

loop = asyncio.get_event_loop()          ❶
task = loop.create_task(main())          ❷
loop.run_until_complete(task)            ❸
pending = asyncio.all_tasks(loop=loop)
for task in pending:
    task.cancel()
group = asyncio.gather(*pending, return_exceptions=True)   ❹
loop.run_until_complete(group)           ❸
loop.close()                             ❺
```

❶ `loop = asyncio.get_event_loop()`

You need a loop instance before you can run any coroutines, and this is how you get one. In fact, anywhere you call it, `get_event_loop()` will give you the same loop instance each time, as long as you're using only a single thread.[2] If you're inside an `async def` function, you should call `asyncio.get_running_loop()` instead, which always gives you what you expect. This is covered in much more detail later in the book.

❷ `task = loop.create_task(coro)`

In this case, the specific call is `loop.create_task(main())`. Your coroutine function will not be executed until you do this. We say that `create_task()` *schedules* your coroutine to be run on the loop.[3] The returned `task` object can be used to monitor the status of the task (for example, whether it is still running or has completed), and can also be used to obtain a result value from your completed coroutine. You can cancel the task with `task.cancel()`.

❸ `loop.run_until_complete(coro)`

This call will *block* the current thread, which will usually be the main thread.

---

2 The asyncio API lets you do lots of wild things with multiple loop instances and threads, but this is not the right book to get into that. 99% of the time you're going to use only a single, main thread for your app, as shown here.

3 Using the parameter name *coro* is a common convention in the API documentation. It refers to a *coroutine*; i.e., strictly speaking, the *result* of calling an async def function, and *not* the function itself.

Note that `run_until_complete()` will keep the loop running only until the given *coro* completes—but all *other* tasks scheduled on the loop will also run while the loop is running. Internally, `asyncio.run()` calls `run_until_complete()` for you and therefore blocks the main thread in the same way.

❹ `group = asyncio.gather(task1, task2, task3)`
When the "main" part of the program unblocks, either due to a process signal (*https://oreil.ly/KfOmB*) being received or the loop being stopped by some code calling `loop.stop()`, the code after `run_until_complete()` will run. The standard idiom as shown here is to gather the still-pending tasks, cancel them, and then use `loop.run_until_complete()` again until those tasks are done. `gather()` is the method for doing the gathering. Note that `asyncio.run()` will do all of the cancelling, gathering, and waiting for pending tasks to finish up.

❺ `loop.close()`
`loop.close()` is usually the final action: it must be called on a stopped loop, and it will clear all queues and shut down the executor. A *stopped* loop can be restarted, but a *closed* loop is gone for good. Internally, `asyncio.run()` will close the loop before returning. This is fine because `run()` creates a new event loop every time you call it.

Example 3-1 shows that if you use `asyncio.run()`, none of these steps are necessary: they are all done for you. However, it is important to understand these steps because more complex situations will come up in practice, and you'll need the extra knowledge to deal with them. Several of these are covered in detail later in the book.

 The preceding example is still too simplistic to be useful in a practical setting. More information around correct shutdown handling is required. The goal of the example is merely to introduce the most important functions and methods in `asyncio`. More practical information for shutdown handling is presented in "Starting Up and Shutting Down (Gracefully!)" on page 57.

`asyncio` in Python exposes a great deal of the underlying machinery around the event loop—and requires you to be aware of aspects like lifecycle management. This is different from Node.js, for example, which also contains an event loop but keeps it somewhat hidden away. However, once you've worked with `asyncio` for bit, you'll begin to notice that the pattern for starting up and shutting down the event loop doesn't stray terribly far from the code presented here. We'll examine some of the nuances of managing the loop life cycle in more detail later in the book.

I left something out in the preceding example. The last item of basic functionality you'll need to know about is how to run *blocking* functions. The thing about

cooperative multitasking is that you need all I/O-bound functions to...well, cooper-
ate, and that means allowing a context switch back to the loop using the keyword
await. Most of the Python code available in the wild today does not do this, and
instead relies on you to run such functions in threads. Until there is more widespread
support for async def functions, you're going to find that using such blocking libraries is unavoidable.

For this, asyncio provides an API that is very similar to the API in the concur
rent.futures package. This package provides a ThreadPoolExecutor and a Proces
sPoolExecutor. The default is thread-based, but either thread-based or pool-based
executors can be used. I omitted executor considerations from the previous example
because they would have obscured the description of how the fundamental parts fit
together. Now that those have been covered, we can look at the executor directly.

There are a couple of quirks to be aware of. Let's have a look at the code sample in
Example 3-3.

Example 3-3. The basic executor interface

```
# quickstart_exe.py
import time
import asyncio

async def main():
    print(f'{time.ctime()} Hello!')
    await asyncio.sleep(1.0)
    print(f'{time.ctime()} Goodbye!')

def blocking():   ❶
    time.sleep(0.5)   ❷
    print(f"{time.ctime()} Hello from a thread!")

loop = asyncio.get_event_loop()
task = loop.create_task(main())

loop.run_in_executor(None, blocking)   ❸
loop.run_until_complete(task)

pending = asyncio.all_tasks(loop=loop)   ❹
for task in pending:
    task.cancel()
group = asyncio.gather(*pending, return_exceptions=True)
loop.run_until_complete(group)
loop.close()
```

❶ blocking() calls the traditional time.sleep() internally, which *would have*
    blocked the main thread and prevented your event loop from running. This
    means that you must not make this function a coroutine—indeed, you cannot

even call this function from *anywhere* in the main thread, which is where the `asyncio` loop is running. We solve this problem by running this function in an *executor*.

❷ Unrelated to this section, but something to keep in mind for later in the book: note that the blocking sleep time (0.5 seconds) is shorter than the nonblocking sleep time (1 second) in the `main()` coroutine. This makes the code sample neat and tidy. In "Waiting for the Executor During Shutdown" on page 68 we'll explore what happens if executor functions outlive their async counterparts during the shutdown sequence.

❸ `await loop.run_in_executor(None, func)`
This is the last of our list of essential, must-know features of `asyncio`. Sometimes you need to run things in a separate thread or even a separate process: this method is used for exactly that. Here we pass our blocking function to be run in the default executor.[4] Note that `run_in_executor()` does *not* block the main thread: it only schedules the executor task to run (it returns a `Future`, which means you can `await` it if the method is called within another coroutine function). The executor task will begin executing only after `run_until_complete()` is called, which allows the event loop to start processing events.

❹ Further to the note in callout 2: the set of tasks in `pending` does *not* include an entry for the call to `blocking()` made in `run_in_executor()`. This will be true of any call that returns a `Future` rather than a `Task`. The documentation is quite good at specifying return types, so you'll see the return type there; just remember that `all_tasks()` really does return only `Tasks`, not `Futures`.

Here's the output of running this script:

```
$ python quickstart_exe.py
Sun Aug 18 01:20:42 2019 Hello!
Sun Aug 18 01:20:43 2019 Hello from a thread!
Sun Aug 18 01:20:43 2019 Goodbye!
```

Now that you've seen the most essential parts of `asyncio` for end-user developer needs, it's time to expand our scope and arrange the `asyncio` API into a kind of hierarchy. This will make it easier to digest and understand how to take what you need from the documentation, and no more.

---

4 Unfortunately, the first parameter of run_in_executor() is the Executor instance to use, and you *must* pass None in order to use the default. Every time I use this, it feels like the "executor" parameter is crying out to be a kwarg with a default value of None.

The Tower of Asyncio

As you saw in the preceding section, there are only a handful of commands that you need to know to be able to use `asyncio` as an end-user developer. Unfortunately, the documentation for `asyncio` presents a huge number of APIs, and it does so in a very "flat" format that makes it hard to tell which things are intended for common use and which are facilities being provided to framework designers.

When framework designers look at the same documentation, they look for *hook points* to which they can connect up their new frameworks or third-party libraries. In this section, we'll look at `asyncio` through the eyes of a framework designer to get a sense of how they might approach building a new async-compatible library. Hopefully, this will help to further delineate the features that you need to care about in your own work.

From this perspective, it is much more useful to think about the `asyncio` module as being arranged in a hierarchy (rather than a flat list), in which each level is built on top of the specification of the previous level. It isn't quite as neat as that, unfortunately, and I've taken liberties with the arrangement in Table 3-1, but hopefully this will give you an alternative view of the `asyncio` API.

Table 3-1, and the names and numbering of the "tiers" given here, is entirely my own invention, intended to add a little structure to help explain the `asyncio` API. The expert reader might arrange things in a different order, and that's OK!

Table 3-1. Features of asyncio arranged in a hierarchy; for end-user developers, the most important tiers are highlighted in bold

Level	Concept	Implementation
Tier 9	**Network: streams**	`StreamReader`, `StreamWriter`, `asyncio.open_connection()`, `asyncio.start_server()`
Tier 8	Network: TCP & UDP	`Protocol`
Tier 7	Network: transports	`BaseTransport`
Tier 6	**Tools**	`asyncio.Queue`
Tier 5	**Subprocesses & threads**	`run_in_executor()`, `asyncio.subprocess`
Tier 4	Tasks	`asyncio.Task`, `asyncio.create_task()`
Tier 3	Futures	`asyncio.Future`
Tier 2	**Event loop**	`asyncio.run()`, `BaseEventLoop`
Tier 1 (Base)	**Coroutines**	`async def`, `async with`, `async for`, `await`

At the most fundamental level, Tier 1, we have the coroutines that you've already seen earlier in this book. This is the lowest level at which one can begin to think about designing a third-party framework, and surprisingly, this turns out to be somewhat popular with not one, but *two*, async frameworks currently available in the wild: Curio (*https://oreil.ly/Zu0lP*) and Trio (*https://oreil.ly/z2lZY*). Both of these rely *only* on native coroutines in Python, and nothing whatsoever from the asyncio library module.

The next level is the event loop. Coroutines are not useful by themselves: they won't do anything without a loop on which to run them (therefore, necessarily, Curio and Trio implement their own event loops). asyncio provides both a loop *specification*, AbstractEventLoop, and an *implementation*, BaseEventLoop.

The clear separation between specification and implementation makes it possible for third-party developers to make alternative implementations of the event loop, and this has already happened with the uvloop (*https://oreil.ly/2itn_*) project, which provides a much faster loop implementation than the one in the asyncio standard library module. Importantly, uvloop simply "plugs into" the hierarchy and replaces *only* the loop part of the stack. The ability to make these kinds of choices is exactly why the asyncio API has been designed like this, with clear separation between the moving parts.

Tiers 3 and 4 bring us futures and tasks, which are very closely related; they're separated only because Task is a subclass of Future, but they could easily be considered to be in the same tier. A Future instance represents some sort of ongoing action that will return a result via *notification* on the event loop, while a Task represents a coroutine running on the event loop. The short version is: a future is "loop-aware," while a task is both "loop-aware" *and* "coroutine-aware." As an end-user developer, you will be working with tasks much more than futures, but for a framework designer, the proportion might be the other way around, depending on the details.

Tier 5 represents the facilities for launching, and awaiting on work that must be run in a separate thread, or even in a separate process.

Tier 6 represents additional async-aware tools such as asyncio.Queue. I could have placed this tier after the network tiers, but I think it's neater to get all of the coroutine-aware APIs out of the way first, before we look at the I/O layers. The Queue provided by asyncio has a very similar API to the thread-safe Queue in the queue module, except that the asyncio version requires the await keyword on get() and put(). You cannot use queue.Queue directly inside coroutines because its get() will block the main thread.

Finally, we have the network I/O tiers, 7 through 9. As an end-user developer, the most convenient API to work with is the streams API at Tier 9. I have positioned the streams API at the highest level of abstraction in the tower. The protocols API, immediately below that (Tier 8), is a more fine-grained API; you *can* use the protocols tier in all instances where you might use the streams tier, but using streams will be simpler. The final network I/O tier is the transport tier (Tier 7). It is unlikely you will ever have to work with this tier directly, unless you're creating a framework for others to use and you need to customize how the transports are set up.

In "Quickstart" on page 22, we looked at the absolute bare minimum that one would need to know to get started with the asyncio library. Now that we've had a look at how the entire asyncio library API is put together, I'd like to revisit that short list of features and reemphasize which parts you are likely to need to learn.

These are the tiers that are most important to focus on when learning how to use the asyncio library module for writing network applications:

Tier 1

Understanding how to write async def functions and use await to call and execute other coroutines is essential.

Tier 2

Understanding how to start up, shut down, and interact with the event loop is essential.

Tier 5

Executors are necessary to use blocking code in your async application, and the reality is that most third-party libraries are not yet asyncio-compatible. A good example of this is the SQLAlchemy database ORM library, for which no feature-comparable alternative is available right now for asyncio.

Tier 6

If you need to feed data to one or more long-running coroutines, the best way to do that is with asyncio.Queue. This is exactly the same strategy as using queue.Queue for distributing data between threads. The Asyncio version of Queue uses the same API as the standard library queue module, but uses coroutines instead of the blocking methods like get().

Tier 9

The streams API gives you the simplest way to handle socket communication over a network, and it is here that you should begin prototyping ideas for network applications. You may find that more fine-grained control is needed, and then you could switch to the protocols API, but in most projects it's usually best to keep things simple until you know exactly what problem you're trying to solve.

Of course, if you're using an asyncio-compatible third-party library that handles all the socket communication for you, like aiohttp, you won't need to directly work with the `asyncio` network tiers at all. In this case, you must rely heavily on the documentation provided with the library.

The `asyncio` library tries to provide sufficient features for both end-user developers and framework designers. Unfortunately, this means that the `asyncio` API can appear somewhat sprawling. I hope that this section has provided enough of a road map to help you pick out the parts you need.

In the next sections, we're going to look at the component parts of the preceding list in more detail.

The pysheeet (*http://bit.ly/2toWDL1*) site provides an in-depth summary (or "cheat sheet") of large chunks of the `asyncio` API; each concept is presented with a short code snippet. The presentation is dense, so I wouldn't recommend it for beginners, but if you have experience with Python and you're the kind of person who "gets it" only when new programming info is presented in code, this is sure to be a useful resource.

Coroutines

Let's begin at the very beginning: what is a coroutine?

My goal in this section is to help you understand the specific meaning behind terms like *coroutine object* and *asynchronous function*. The examples that follow will show low-level interactions not normally required in most programs; however, the examples will help give you a clearer understanding of the fundamental parts of Asyncio, and will make later sections much easier to grasp.

The following examples can all be reproduced in a Python 3.8 interpreter in interactive mode, and I urge you to work through them on your own by typing them yourself, observing the output, and perhaps experimenting with different ways of interacting with `async` and `await`.

asyncio was first added to Python 3.4, but the new syntax for coroutines using `async def` and `await` was only added in Python 3.5. How did people do anything with `asyncio` in 3.4? They used *generators* in very special ways to act as if they were coroutines. In some older codebases, you'll see generator functions decorated with `@asyncio.coroutine` and containing `yield from` statements. Coroutines created with the newer `async def` are now referred to as *native coroutines* because they are built into the language as coroutines and nothing else. This book ignores the older generator-based coroutines entirely.

The New async def Keywords

Let us begin with the simplest possible thing, shown in Example 3-4.

Example 3-4. Async functions are functions, not coroutines

```
>>> async def f():    ❶
...     return 123
...
>>> type(f)   ❷
<class 'function'>
>>> import inspect   ❸
>>> inspect.iscoroutinefunction(f)   ❹
True
```

❶ This is the simplest possible declaration of a coroutine: it looks like a regular function, except that it begins with the keywords `async def`.

❷ Surprise! The precise type of f is *not* "coroutine"; it's just an ordinary function. While it is common to refer to `async def` functions as coroutines, strictly speaking they are considered by Python to be *coroutine functions*. This behavior is identical to the way generator functions work in Python:

```
>>> def g():
...     yield 123
...
>>> type(g)
<class 'function'>
>>> gen = g()
>>> type(gen)
<class 'generator'>
```

Even though g is sometimes incorrectly referred to as a "generator," it remains a function, and it is only when this function is *evaluated* that the generator is returned. Coroutine functions work in exactly the same way: you need to *call* the `async def` function to obtain the coroutine object.

❸ The `inspect` module in the standard library can provide much better introspective capabilities than the `type()` built-in function.

❹ There is an `iscoroutinefunction()` function that lets you distinguish between an ordinary function and a coroutine function.

Returning to our `async def f()`, Example 3-5 reveals what happens when we call it.

Example 3-5. An async def function returns a coroutine object

```
>>> coro = f()
>>> type(coro)
<class 'coroutine'>
>>> inspect.iscoroutine(coro)
True
```

This brings us back to our original question: what exactly is a coroutine? A *coroutine* is an *object* that encapsulates the ability to resume an underlying function that has been suspended before completion. If that sounds familiar, it's because coroutines are very similar to generators. Indeed, before the introduction of *native* coroutines with the async def and await keywords in Python 3.5, it was already possible to use the asyncio library in Python 3.4 by using normal generators with special decorators.[5] It isn't surprising that the new async def functions (and the coroutines they return) behave in a similar way to generators.

We can play with coroutine objects a bit more to see how Python makes use of them. Most importantly, we want to see how Python is able to "switch" execution between coroutines. Let's first look at how the return value can be obtained.

When a coroutine *returns*, what really happens is that a StopIteration exception is raised. Example 3-6, which continues in the same session as the previous examples, makes that clear.

Example 3-6. Coroutine internals: using send() and StopIteration

```
>>> async def f():
...     return 123
>>> coro = f()
>>> try:
...     coro.send(None)    ❶
... except StopIteration as e:
...     print('The answer was:', e.value)    ❷
...
The answer was: 123
```

❶ A coroutine is *initiated* by "sending" it a None. Internally, this is what the *event loop* is going to be doing to your precious coroutines; you will never have to do this manually. All the coroutines you make will be executed either with loop.create_task(*coro*) or await *coro*. It's the loop that does the .send(None) behind the scenes.

---

5 And furthermore, this is how other open source libraries such as Twisted and Tornado have exposed async support in the past.

❷ When the coroutine *returns*, a special kind of exception is raised, called `StopIter` `ation`. Note that we can access the return value of the coroutine via the `value` attribute of the exception itself. Again, you don't need to know that it works like this: from your point of view, `async def` functions will simply return a value with the `return` statement, just like normal functions.

These two points, the `send()` and the `StopIteration`, define the start and end of the executing coroutine, respectively. So far this just seems like a really convoluted way to run a function, but that's OK: the *event loop* will be responsible for driving coroutines with these low-level internals. From your point of view, you will simply schedule coroutines for execution on the loop, and they will get executed top-down, almost like normal functions.

The next step is to see how the execution of the coroutine can be suspended.

The New await Keyword

This new keyword `await` (*https://oreil.ly/uk4H3*) always takes a parameter and will accept *only* a thing called an *awaitable*, which is defined as one of these (exclusively!):

- A coroutine (i.e., the *result* of a called `async def` function).[6]

- Any object implementing the __await__() special method. That special method *must* return an iterator.

The second kind of awaitable is out of scope for this book (you'll never need it in day-to-day `asyncio` programming), but the first use case is pretty straightforward, as Example 3-7 shows.

Example 3-7. Using await on a coroutine

```
async def f():
    await asyncio.sleep(1.0)
    return 123

async def main():
    result = await f()   ❶
    return result
```

❶ Calling `f()` produces a coroutine; this means we are allowed to `await` it. The value of the `result` variable will be `123` when `f()` completes.

---

6 Also acceptable is a legacy, generator-based coroutine, which is a generator function that is decorated with `@types.coroutine` and uses the `yield from` keyword internally to suspend. We are going to completely ignore legacy coroutines in this book. Erase them from your mind!

Before we close out this section and move on to the event loop, it is useful to look at how coroutines may be fed exceptions. This is most commonly used for cancellation: when you call task.cancel(), the event loop will internally use coro.throw() to raise asyncio.CancelledError *inside* your coroutine (Example 3-8).

Example 3-8. Using coro.throw() to inject exceptions into a coroutine

```
>>> coro = f()  ❶
>>> coro.send(None)
>>> coro.throw(Exception, 'blah')  ❷
Traceback (most recent call last):
  File "<stdin>", line 1, in <module>
  File "<stdin>", line 2, in f
Exception: blah
blah
```

❶ As before, a new coroutine is created from the coroutine function f().

❷ Instead of doing another send(), we call throw() and provide an exception class and a value. This raises an exception *inside* our coroutine, at the await point.

The throw() method is used (internally in asyncio) for *task cancellation*, which we can also demonstrate quite easily. We're even going to go ahead in Example 3-9 and handle the cancellation inside a new coroutine.

Example 3-9. Coroutine cancellation with CancelledError

```
>>> import asyncio
>>> async def f():
...     try:
...         while True: await asyncio.sleep(0)
...     except asyncio.CancelledError:  ❶
...         print('I was cancelled!')  ❷
...     else:
...         return 111
>>> coro = f()
>>> coro.send(None)
>>> coro.send(None)
>>> coro.throw(asyncio.CancelledError)  ❸
I was cancelled!  ❹
Traceback (most recent call last):
  File "<stdin>", line 1, in <module>
StopIteration  ❺
```

❶ Our coroutine function now handles an exception. In fact, it handles the *specific* exception type used throughout the asyncio library for task cancellation: asyncio.CancelledError. Note that the exception is being injected into the coroutine from outside; i.e., by the event loop, which we're still simulating with manual send() and throw() commands. In real code, which you'll see later, CancelledError is raised inside the task-wrapped coroutine when tasks are cancelled.

❷ A simple message to say that the task got cancelled. Note that by handling the exception, we ensure it will no longer propagate and our coroutine will return.

❸ Here we throw() the CancelledError exception.

❹ As expected, we see our cancellation message being printed.

❺ Our coroutine exits normally. (Recall that the StopIteration exception is the normal way that coroutines exit.)

Just to drive home the point about how task cancellation is nothing more than regular exception raising (and handling), let's look at Example 3-10, where we absorb cancellation and move on to a different coroutine.

Example 3-10. For educational purposes only—don't do this!

```
>>> async def f():
...     try:
...         while True: await asyncio.sleep(0)
...     except asyncio.CancelledError:
...         print('Nope!')
...         while True: await asyncio.sleep(0)  ❶
...     else:
...         return 111
>>> coro = f()
>>> coro.send(None)
>>> coro.throw(asyncio.CancelledError)  ❷
Nope!
>>> coro.send(None)  ❸
```

❶ Instead of printing a message, what happens if after cancellation, we just go right back to awaiting another awaitable?

❷ Unsurprisingly, our outer coroutine continues to live, and it immediately suspends again inside the *new* coroutine.

❸ Everything proceeds normally, and our coroutine continues to suspend and resume as expected.

Of course, it should go without saying that you should never actually do this! If your coroutine receives a cancellation signal, that is a clear directive to do only whatever cleanup is necessary and exit. Don't just ignore it.

By this point, it's getting pretty tiring *pretending* to be an event loop by manually doing all the .send(None) calls, so in Example 3-11 we'll bring in the loop provided by asyncio and clean up the preceding example accordingly.

Example 3-11. Using the event loop to execute coroutines

```
>>> async def f():
...     await asyncio.sleep(0)
...     return 111
>>> loop = asyncio.get_event_loop()      ❶
>>> coro = f()
>>> loop.run_until_complete(coro)        ❷
111
```

❶ Obtain a loop.

❷ Run the coroutine to completion. Internally, this is doing all those .send(None) method calls for us, and it detects completion of our coroutine with the StopIteration exception, which also contains our return value.

Event Loop

The preceding section showed how the send() and throw() methods can interact with a coroutine, but that was just to help you understand how coroutines themselves are structured. The event loop in asyncio handles all of the switching between coroutines, as well as catching those StopIteration exceptions—and much more, such as listening to sockets and file descriptors for events.

You can get by without ever needing to work with the event loop directly: your asyncio code can be written entirely using await calls, initiated by an asyncio.run(coro) call. However, at times some degree of interaction with the event loop itself might be necessary, and here we'll discuss how to obtain it.

There are two ways:

Recommended
    asyncio.get_running_loop(), callable from inside the context of a coroutine

Discouraged
    asyncio.get_event_loop(), callable from anywhere

You're going to see the discouraged function in much existing code, because the newer function, `get_running_loop()`, was introduced much later, in Python 3.8. Thus, it will be useful in practice to have a basic idea of how the older method works, so we'll look at both. Let's start with Example 3-12.

Example 3-12. Always getting the same event loop

```
>>> loop = asyncio.get_event_loop()
>>> loop2 = asyncio.get_event_loop()
>>> loop is loop2    ❶
True
```

❶ Both identifiers, `loop` and `loop2`, refer to the same instance.

This means that if you're inside a coroutine function and you need access to the loop instance, it's fine to call `get_event_loop()` or `get_running_loop()` to obtain it. You *do not* need to pass an explicit `loop` parameter through all your functions.

The situation is different if you're a framework designer: it would be better to design your functions to accept a `loop` parameter, just in case your users are doing something unusual with event loop policies (*https://oreil.ly/oMe9w*). Policies are out of scope for this book, and we'll say no more about them.

So if `get_event_loop()` and `get_running_loop()` work the same, why do they both exist? The `get_event_loop()` method works only within the *same thread*. In fact, `get_event_loop()` will fail if called inside a new thread unless you specifically create a new loop with `new_event_loop()`, *and* set that new instance to be *the* loop for that thread by calling `set_event_loop()`. Most of us will only ever need (and want!) a single loop instance running in a single thread. This is nearly the entire point of async programming in the first place.

In contrast, `get_running_loop()` (the recommended method) will always do what you expect: because it can be called only within the context of a coroutine, a task, or a function called from one of those, it always provides the *current* running event loop, which is almost always what you want.

The introduction of `get_running_loop()` has also simplified the spawning of background tasks. Consider Example 3-13, a coroutine function inside which additional tasks are created and *not* awaited.

Example 3-13. Creating tasks

```
async def f():
    # Create some tasks!
    loop = asyncio.get_event_loop()
```

```
for i in range():
    loop.create_task(<some other coro>)
```

In this example, the intention is to launch completely new tasks inside the coroutine. By not awaiting them, we ensure they will run independently of the execution context inside coroutine function f(). In fact, f() will exit before the tasks that it launched have completed.

Before Python 3.7, it was necessary to first obtain the loop instance to schedule a task, but with the introduction of get_running_loop() came other asyncio functions that use it, like asyncio.create_task(). From Python 3.7 on, the code to spawn an async task now looks like Example 3-14.

Example 3-14. Creating tasks the modern way

```
import asyncio

async def f():
    # Create some tasks!
    for i in range():
        asyncio.create_task(<some other coro>)
```

It is also possible to use another low-level function called asyncio.ensure_future() to spawn tasks in the same way as create_task(), and you will likely still see calls to ensure_future() in older asyncio code. I considered avoiding the distraction of discussing ensure_future(), but it is a perfect case study of an asyncio API that was intended only for framework designers, but made the original adoption of asyncio much more difficult to understand for application developers. The difference between asyncio.create_task() and asyncio.ensure_future() is subtle and confusing for many newcomers. We explore these differences in the next section.

Tasks and Futures

Earlier we covered coroutines, and how they need to be run on a loop to be useful. Now I want to talk briefly about the Task and Future APIs. The one you will work with the most is Task, as most of your work will involve running coroutines with the create_task() function, exactly as set out in "Quickstart" on page 22. The Future class is actually a superclass of Task, and it provides all of the functionality for interaction with the loop.

A simple way to think of it is like this: a Future represents a future completion state of some activity and is managed by the loop. A Task is exactly the same, but the specific "activity" is a coroutine— probably one of yours that you created with an async def function plus create_task().

The Future class represents a *state* of something that is interacting with a loop. That description is too fuzzy to be useful, so you can instead think of a Future instance as a toggle for completion status. When a Future instance is created, the toggle is set to "not yet completed," but at some later time it will be "completed." In fact, a Future instance has a method called done() that allows you to check the status, as shown in Example 3-15.

Example 3-15. Checking completion status with done()

```
>>> from asyncio import Future
>>> f = Future()
>>> f.done()
False
```

A Future instance may also do the following:

- Have a "result" value set (use .set_result(*value*) to set it and .result() to obtain it)

- Be cancelled with .cancel() (and check for cancellation with .cancelled())

- Have additional callback functions added that will be run when the future completes

Even though Tasks are more common, you can't avoid Futures entirely: for instance, running a function on an executor will return a Future instance, *not* a Task. Let's take a quick look at Example 3-16 to get a feel for what it is like to work with a Future instance directly.

Example 3-16. Interaction with a Future instance

```
>>> import asyncio
>>>
>>> async def main(f: asyncio.Future):   ❶
...     await asyncio.sleep(1)
...     f.set_result('I have finished.')   ❷
...
>>> loop = asyncio.get_event_loop()
>>> fut = asyncio.Future()   ❸
>>> print(fut.done())   ❹
False
>>> loop.create_task(main(fut))   ❺
<Task pending name='Task-1' coro=<main() running at <console>:1>>
>>> loop.run_until_complete(fut)   ❻
'I have finished.'
>>> print(fut.done())
True
```

```
>>> print(fut.result())  ❼
I have finished.
```

❶ Create a simple `main` function. We can run this, wait for a bit, and then set a result on this `Future`, `f`.

❷ Set the result.

❸ Manually create a `Future` instance. Note that this instance is (by default) tied to our `loop`, but it is not and will not be attached to any coroutine (that's what `Tasks` are for).

❹ Before doing anything, verify that the future is not done yet.

❺ *Schedule* the `main()` coroutine, passing the future. Remember, all the `main()` coroutine does is sleep and then toggle the `Future` instance. (Note that the `main()` coroutine will not start running yet: coroutines run only when the loop is running.)

❻ Here we use `run_until_complete()` on a `Future` instance, rather than a `Task` instance.[7] This is different from what you've seen before. Now that the loop is running, the `main()` coroutine will begin executing.

❼ Eventually, the future completes when its result is set. After completion, the result can be accessed.

Of course, it is unlikely that you will work with `Future` directly in the way shown here; the code sample is for education purposes only. Most of your contact with `asyncio` will be through `Task` instances.

You might wonder what happens if you call `set_result()` on a `Task` instance. It was possible to do this before Python 3.8, but it is no longer allowed. `Task` instances are wrappers for coroutine objects, and their result values can be set only internally as the result of the underlying coroutine function, as shown in Example 3-17.

Example 3-17. Calling set_result() on a Task

```
>>> import asyncio
>>> from contextlib import suppress
```

---

7 The documentation is inconsistent here: the signature is given as `AbstractEventLoop.run_until_com plete(future)`, but it really should be `AbstractEventLoop.run_until_complete(coro_or_future)` as the same rules apply.

```
>>>
>>> async def main(f: asyncio.Future):
...     await asyncio.sleep(1)
...     try:
...         f.set_result('I have finished.')   ❷
...     except RuntimeError as e:
...         print(f'No longer allowed: {e}')
...         f.cancel()   ❸
...
>>> loop = asyncio.get_event_loop()
>>> fut = asyncio.Task(asyncio.sleep(1_000_000))   ❶
>>> print(fut.done())
False
>>> loop.create_task(main(fut))
<Task pending name='Task-2' coro=<main() running at <console>:1>>
>>> with suppress(asyncio.CancelledError):
...     loop.run_until_complete(fut)
...
No longer allowed: Task does not support set_result operation
>>> print(fut.done())
True
>>> print(fut.cancelled())   ❸
True
```

❶ The only difference is that we create a Task instance instead of a Future. Of course, the Task API requires us to provide a coroutine; we just use sleep() because it's convenient.

❷ A Task instance is being passed in. It satisfies the type signature of the function (because Task is a subclass of Future), but since Python 3.8, we're no longer allowed to call set_result() on a Task: an attempt will raise RuntimeError. The idea is that a Task represents a running coroutine, so the result should always come only from that.

❸ We can, however, still cancel() a task, which will raise CancelledError inside the underlying coroutine.

Create a Task? Ensure a Future? Make Up Your Mind!

In "Quickstart" on page 22, I said that the way to run coroutines was to use asyncio.create_task(). Before that function was introduced, it was necessary to obtain a loop instance and use loop.create_task() to do the same thing. This can, in fact, also be achieved with a different module-level function: asyncio.ensure_future(). Some developers recommended create_task(), while others recommended ensure_future().

During my research for this book, I became convinced that the API method `asyncio.ensure_future()` is responsible for much of the widespread misunderstanding about the `asyncio` library. Much of the API is really quite clear, but there are a few bad stumbling blocks to learning, and this is one of them. When you come across `ensure_future()`, your brain works very hard to integrate it into your mental model of how `asyncio` should be used—and likely fails!

The problem with `ensure_future()` is highlighted by this now-infamous explanation in the Python 3.6 `asyncio` documentation (*https://oreil.ly/fnjCs*):

`asyncio.ensure_future(`*coro_or_future*`, *, _loop=None)`

> Schedule the execution of a *coroutine object*: wrap it in a future. Return a *Task* object.
>
> If the argument is a *Future*, it is returned directly.

What!? When I first read this, it was very confusing. Here is a (hopefully) clearer description of `ensure_future()`:

- If you pass in a coroutine, it will produce a `Task` instance (and your coroutine will be scheduled to run on the event loop). This is identical to calling `asyncio.create_task()` (or `loop.create_task()`) and returning the new `Task` instance.

- If you pass in a `Future` instance (or a `Task` instance, because `Task` is a subclass of `Future`), you get that very same thing returned, *unchanged*. Yes, really!

This function is a great example of the difference between the `asyncio` API that is aimed at *end-user developers* (the high-level API) and the `asyncio` API aimed at *framework designers* (the low-level API). Let's have a closer look at how it works, in Example 3-18.

Example 3-18. A closer look at what ensure_future() is doing

```
import asyncio

async def f():    ❶
    pass

coro = f()   ❷
loop = asyncio.get_event_loop()   ❸

task = loop.create_task(coro)   ❹
assert isinstance(task, asyncio.Task)   ❺

new_task = asyncio.ensure_future(coro)   ❻
assert isinstance(new_task, asyncio.Task)
```

```
mystery_meat = asyncio.ensure_future(task)  ❼
assert mystery_meat is task  ❽
```

❶ A simple do-nothing coroutine function. We just need something that can make a coroutine.

❷ We make the coroutine object by calling the function directly. Your code will rarely do this, but I want to be explicit here (a few lines down) that we're passing a coroutine object into each of `create_task()` and `ensure_future()`.

❸ Obtain the loop.

❹ First off, we use `loop.create_task()` to schedule our coroutine on the loop, and we get a new `Task` instance back.

❺ We verify the type. So far, nothing interesting.

❻ We show that `asyncio.ensure_future()` can be used to perform the same act as `create_task()`: we passed in a coroutine and we got back a `Task` instance (and the coroutine has been scheduled to run on the loop)! If you're passing in a coroutine, there is no difference between `loop.create_task()` and `asyncio.ensure_future()`.

❼ But what happens if we pass a `Task` instance to `ensure_future()`? Note that we're passing in a `Task` instance that was already created by `loop.create_task()` in step 4.

❽ We get back *exactly* the same `Task` instance as we passed in: it passes through unchanged.

What's the point of passing `Future` instances straight through? And why do two different things with the same function? The answer is that `ensure_future()` is intended to be used *by framework authors* to provide APIs *to end-user developers* that can handle both kinds of parameters. Don't believe me? Here it is from the ex-BDFL himself:

> The point of `ensure_future()` is if you have something that could either be a coroutine or a `Future` (the latter includes a `Task` because that's a subclass of `Future`), and you want to be able to call a method on it that is only defined on `Future` (probably about the only useful example being `cancel()`). When it is already a `Future` (or `Task`), this does nothing; when it is a coroutine, it wraps it in a `Task`.

> If you know that you have a coroutine and you want it to be scheduled, the correct API to use is `create_task()`. The only time when you should be calling `ensure_future()` is when you are providing an API (like most of asyncio's own APIs) that accepts either

a coroutine or a Future and you need to do something to it that requires you to have a Future.

—Guido van Rossum, commenting (*https://oreil.ly/cSOFB*) on issue #477 (*https:// oreil.ly/ydRpR*)

In sum, `asyncio.ensure_future()` is a helper function intended for framework designers. This is easiest to explain by analogy to a much more common kind of function, so let's do that. If you have a few years' programming experience behind you, you may have seen functions similar to the `listify()` function in Example 3-19.

Example 3-19. A utility function for coercing input into a list

```
def listify(x: Any) -> List:
    """ Try hard to convert x into a list """
    if isinstance(x, (str, bytes)):
        return [x]

    try:
        return [_ for _ in x]
    except TypeError:
        return [x]
```

This function tries to convert the argument into a list, no matter what comes in. These kinds of functions are often used in APIs and frameworks to coerce inputs into a known type, which simplifies subsequent code—in this case, you know that the parameter (output from `listify()`) will always be a list.

If I rename the `listify()` function to `ensure_list()`, then you should begin to see the parallel with `asyncio.ensure_future()`: it tries to always coerce the argument into a Future (or subclass) type. This is a utility function to make life easier for *framework developers*, not end-user developers like you and I.

Indeed, the `asyncio` standard library module itself uses `ensure_future()` for exactly this reason. When next you look over the API, everywhere you see a function parameter described as "awaitable objects," it is likely that internally `ensure_future()` is being used to coerce the parameter. For example, the `asyncio.gather()` function has the following signature:

```
asyncio.gather(*aws, loop=None, ...)
```

The *aws* parameter means "awaitable objects," which includes coroutines, tasks, and futures. Internally, `gather()` is using `ensure_future()` for type coercion: tasks and futures are left untouched, while tasks are created for coroutines.

The key point here is that as an end-user application developer, you should never need to use `asyncio.ensure_future()`. It's more a tool for framework designers. If you need to schedule a coroutine on the event loop, just do that directly with `asyncio.create_task()`.

In the next few sections, we'll go back to language-level features, starting with asynchronous context managers.

Async Context Managers: async with

Support for coroutines in context managers turns out to be exceptionally convenient. This makes sense, because many situations require network resources—say, connections—to be opened and closed within a well-defined scope.

The key to understanding `async with` is to realize that the operation of a context manager is driven by *method calls*, and then consider: what if those methods were coroutine functions? Indeed, this is exactly how it works, as shown in Example 3-20.

Example 3-20. Async context manager

```
class Connection:
    def __init__(self, host, port):
        self.host = host
        self.port = port
    async def __aenter__(self):       ❶
        self.conn = await get_conn(self.host, self.port)
        return conn
    async def __aexit__(self, exc_type, exc, tb):       ❷
        await self.conn.close()

async with Connection('localhost', 9001) as conn:
    <do stuff with conn>
```

❶ Instead of the __enter__() special method for synchronous context managers, the new __aenter__() special method is used. This special method must be an `async def` method.

❷ Likewise, instead of __exit__(), use __aexit__(). The parameters are identical to those for __exit__() and are populated if an exception was raised in the body of the context manager.

> Just because you're using `asyncio` in your program, that doesn't mean that all your context managers must be async ones like these. They're useful only if you need to `await` something inside the *enter* and *exit* methods. If there is no blocking I/O code, just use regular context managers.

Now—between you and me—I don't much like using this explicit style of context manager when the wonderful @contextmanager decorator exists in the contextlib module of the standard library. As you might guess, an asynchronous version, @asynccontextmanager, also exists and makes it much easier to create simple async context managers.

The contextlib Way

This approach is analogous to the @contextmanager decorator in the contextlib standard library. To recap, Example 3-21 takes a look at the blocking way first.

Example 3-21. The blocking way

```
from contextlib import contextmanager

@contextmanager   ❶
def web_page(url):
    data = download_webpage(url)   ❷
    yield data
    update_stats(url)   ❸

with web_page('google.com') as data:   ❹
    process(data)   ❺
```

❶ The @contextmanager decorator transforms a generator function into a context manager.

❷ This function call (which I made up for this example) looks suspiciously like the sort of thing that will want to use a network interface, which is many orders of magnitude slower than "normal" CPU-bound code. This context manager *must* be used in a dedicated thread; otherwise, the whole program will be paused while waiting for data.

❸ Imagine that we update some statistics every time we process data from a URL, such as the number of times the URL has been downloaded. From a concurrency perspective, we would need to know whether this function involves I/O internally, such as writing to a database over a network. If so, update_stats() is also a blocking call.

❹ Our context manager is being used. Note specifically how the network call (to download_webpage()) is hidden inside the construction of the context manager.

❺ This function call, process(), might also be blocking. We'd have to look at what the function does, because the distinction between what is blocking or nonblocking is not clear-cut. It might be:

- Innocuous and nonblocking (fast and CPU-bound)
- Mildly blocking (fast and I/O-bound, perhaps something like fast disk access instead of network I/O)
- Blocking (slow and I/O-bound)
- Diabolical (slow and CPU-bound)

For the sake of simplicity in this example, let's presume that the call to process() is a fast, CPU-bound operation and therefore nonblocking.

Example 3-22 is exactly the same example, but using the new async-aware helper that was introduced in Python 3.7.

Example 3-22. The nonblocking way

```
from contextlib import asynccontextmanager

@asynccontextmanager     ❶
async def web_page(url):     ❷
    data = await download_webpage(url)     ❸
    yield data     ❹
    await update_stats(url)     ❺

async with web_page('google.com') as data:     ❻
    process(data)
```

❶ The new @asynccontextmanager decorator is used in exactly the same way.

❷ It does, however, require that the decorated generator function be declared with async def.

❸ As before, we fetch the data from the URL before making it available to the body of the context manager. I have added the await keyword, which tells us that this coroutine will allow the event loop to run other tasks while we wait for the network call to complete.

Note that we *cannot* simply tack on the await keyword to anything. This change presupposes that we were also able to *modify* the download_webpage() function itself, and convert it into a coroutine that is compatible with the await keyword. For the times when it is not possible to modify the function, a different approach is needed; we'll discuss that in the next example.

❹ As before, the data is made available to the body of the context manager. I'm trying to keep the code simple, so I've omitted the usual try/finally handler that you should normally write to deal with exceptions raised in the body of caller.

Note that the presence of `yield` is what changes a function into a *generator function*; the additional presence of the `async def` keywords in point 1 makes this an *asynchronous generator function*. When called, it will return an *asynchronous generator*. The `inspect` module has two functions that can test for these: `isasyncgenfunction()` and `isasyncgen()`, respectively.

❺ Here, assume that we've also converted the code inside the `update_stats()` function to allow it to produce coroutines. We can then use the `await` keyword, which allows a context switch to the event loop while we wait for the I/O-bound work to complete.

❻ Another change was required in the usage of the context manager itself: we needed to use `async with` instead of a plain `with`.

Hopefully, this example shows that the new `@asynccontextmanager` is perfectly analogous to the `@contextmanager` decorator.

In callouts 3 and 5, I said it was necessary to modify some functions to return coroutines; these were `download_webpage()` and `update_stats()`. This is usually not that easy to do, since async support needs to be added down at the socket level. The focus of the preceding examples was simply to show off the new `@asynccontextmanager` decorator, not to show how to convert blocking functions into nonblocking ones. The more common situation is when you want to use a blocking function in your program, but it's not possible to modify the code in that function.

This situation will usually happen with third-party libraries, and a great example is the `requests` library, which uses blocking calls throughout.[8] If you can't change the code being called, there is another way. This is a convenient place to show you how an *executor* can be used to do exactly that, as illustrated in Example 3-23.

Example 3-23. The nonblocking-with-a-little-help-from-my-friends way

```
from contextlib import asynccontextmanager

@asynccontextmanager
async def web_page(url):        ❶
    loop = asyncio.get_event_loop()
    data = await loop.run_in_executor(
        None, download_webpage, url)   ❷
```

---

8 Async support can be quite difficult to add to an existing framework after the fact since large structural changes to the codebase might be needed. This was discussed in a GitHub issue for `requests` (*https://oreil.ly/we5cZ*).

```
    yield data
    await loop.run_in_executor(None, update_stats, url)  ❸

async with web_page('google.com') as data:
    process(data)
```

❶ For this example, assume that we are *unable* to modify the code for our two
   blocking calls, `download_webpage()` and `update_stats()`; i.e., we can't alter
   them to be coroutine functions. That's bad, because the most grave sin of event-
   based programming is breaking the rule that you must never, under any circum-
   stances, prevent the event loop from processing events.

   To get around the problem, we will use an *executor* to run the blocking calls in a
   separate thread. The executor is made available to us as an attribute of the event
   loop itself.

❷ We call the executor. The signature is `AbstractEventLoop.run_in_execu`
   `tor(executor, func, *args)`. If you want to use the default executor (which is a
   `ThreadPoolExecutor`), you must pass `None` as the value for the *executor*
   argument.[9]

❸ As with the call to `download_webpage()`, we also run the other blocking call to
   `update_stats()` in an executor. Note that you *must* use the `await` keyword in
   front. If you forget, the execution of the asynchronous generator (i.e., your async
   context manager) will not wait for the call to complete before proceeding.

It's likely that async context managers are going to be heavily used in many `asyncio`-
based codebases, so it's pretty important to have a good understanding of them. You
can read more about the new `@asynccontextmanager` decorator in the Python 3.7
documentation (*http://bit.ly/2FoWl9f*).

Async Iterators: async for

Next up is the async version of the `for` loop. It is easiest to understand how this works
if you first recognize that ordinary iteration—just like so many other language features—is implemented through the use of *special methods*, recognizable by the double
underscores in their names.

For reference, Example 3-24 shows how a standard (nonasync) iterator is defined
through the use of the __iter__() and __next__() methods.

---

9 Yes, this is super annoying. Every time I use this call, I can't help wondering why the more common idiom of
  using executor=None as a keyword argument was not preferred.

Example 3-24. A traditional, nonasync iterator

```
>>> class A:
...     def __iter__(self):      ❶
...         self.x = 0           ❷
...         return self          ❸
...     def __next__(self):      ❹
...         if self.x > 2:
...             raise StopIteration   ❺
...         else:
...             self.x += 1
...             return self.x    ❻
>>> for i in A():
...     print(i)
1
2
3
```

❶ An *iterator* must implement the __iter__() special method.

❷ Initialize some state to the "starting" state.

❸ The __iter__() special method must return an *iterable*; i.e., an object that implements the __next__() special method. In this case, it's the same instance, because A itself also implements the __next__() special method.

❹ The __next__() method is defined. This will be called for every step in the iteration sequence until…

❺ …StopIteration is raised.

❻ The *returned values* for each iteration are generated.

Now you ask: what happens if you declare the __next__() special method as an async def coroutine function? That will allow it to await some kind of I/O-bound operation—and this is pretty much exactly how async for works, except for some small details around naming. The specification (in PEP 492) shows that to use async for on an async iterator, several things are required in the async iterator itself:

1. You must implement def __aiter__(). (Note: *not* with async def!)

2. __aiter__() must return an object that implements async def __anext__().

3. __anext__() must return a value for each iteration and raise StopAsync Iteration when finished.

Let's take a quick look at how that might work. Imagine that we have a bunch of keys in a Redis (*https://redis.io/*) database, and we want to iterate over their data, but we fetch the data only on demand. An asynchronous iterator for that might look like Example 3-25.

Example 3-25. Async iterator for fetching data from Redis

```
import asyncio
from aioredis import create_redis

async def main():                                      ❶
    redis = await create_redis(('localhost', 6379))    ❷
    keys = ['Americas', 'Africa', 'Europe', 'Asia']    ❸

    async for value in OneAtATime(redis, keys):        ❹
        await do_something_with(value)                 ❺

class OneAtATime:
    def __init__(self, redis, keys):                   ❻
        self.redis = redis
        self.keys = keys
    def __aiter__(self):                               ❼
        self.ikeys = iter(self.keys)
        return self
    async def __anext__(self):                         ❽
        try:
            k = next(self.ikeys)                       ❾
        except StopIteration:                          ❿
            raise StopAsyncIteration

        value = await redis.get(k)                     ⓫
        return value

asyncio.run(main())
```

❶ The main() function: we run it using asyncio.run() toward the bottom of the code sample.

❷ We use the high-level interface in aioredis to get a connection.

❸ Imagine that each of the values associated with these keys is quite large and stored in the Redis instance.

❹ We're using async for: the point is that *iteration is able to suspend itself* while waiting for the next datum to arrive.

❺ For completeness, imagine that we also perform some I/O-bound activity on the fetched value—perhaps a simple data transformation—and then it gets sent on to another destination.

❻ The initializer of this class is quite ordinary: we store the Redis connection instance and the list of keys to iterate over.

❼ Just as in the previous code example with `__iter__()`, we use `__aiter__()` to set things up for iteration. We create a normal iterator over the keys, `self.ikeys`, and `return self` because `OneAtATime` also implements the `__anext__()` coroutine method.

❽ Note that the `__anext__()` method is declared with `async def`, while the `__aiter__()` method is declared only with `def`.

❾ For each key, we fetch the value from Redis: `self.ikeys` is a regular iterator over the keys, so we use `next()` to move over them.

❿ When `self.ikeys` is exhausted, we handle the `StopIteration` and simply turn it into a `StopAsyncIteration`! This is how you signal stop from inside an async iterator.

⓫ Finally—the entire point of this example—we can get the data from Redis associated with this key. We can `await` the data, which means that other code can run on the event loop while we wait on network I/O.

Hopefully, this example is clear: `async for` provides the ability to retain the convenience of a simple `for` loop, even when iterating over data where the iteration itself is performing I/O. The benefit is that you can process enormous amounts of data with a single loop, because you have to deal with each chunk only in tiny batches.

Simpler Code with Async Generators

Async generators are `async def` functions that have `yield` keywords inside them. Async generators result in simpler code.

However, the idea of them might be confusing if you have some experience with using generators *as if* they were coroutines, such as with the Twisted framework, or the Tornado framework, or even with `yield from` in Python 3.4's `asyncio`. Therefore, before we continue, it will be best if you can convince yourself that

- Coroutines and generators are completely different concepts.
- Async generators behave much like ordinary generators.

- For iteration, you use `async for` for async generators, instead of the ordinary `for` used for ordinary generators.

The example used in the previous section to demonstrate an async iterator for inter-action with Redis turns out to be much simpler if we set it up as an async generator, shown in Example 3-26.

Example 3-26. Easier with an async generator

```python
import asyncio
from aioredis import create_redis

async def main():                                           ❶
    redis = await create_redis(('localhost', 6379))
    keys = ['Americas', 'Africa', 'Europe', 'Asia']

    async for value in one_at_a_time(redis, keys):          ❷
        await do_something_with(value)

async def one_at_a_time(redis, keys):                       ❸
    for k in keys:
        value = await redis.get(k)      ❹
        yield value      ❺

asyncio.run(main())
```

❶ The `main()` function is identical to the version in Example 3-25.

❷ Well, almost identical: I changed the name from *CamelCase* to *snake_case*.

❸ Our function is now declared with `async def`, making it a *coroutine function*, and since this function also contains the `yield` keyword, we refer to it as an *asynchronous generator function*.

❹ We don't have to do the convoluted things necessary in the previous example with `self.ikeys`: here, we just loop over the keys directly and obtain the value…

❺ …and then yield it to the caller, just like a normal generator.

It might seem complex if this is new to you, but I urge you to play around with this yourself on a few toy examples. It starts to feel natural pretty quickly. Async generators are likely to become popular in `asyncio`-based codebases because they bring all the same benefits as normal generators: making code shorter and simpler.

Async Comprehensions

Now that we've seen how Python supports asynchronous iteration, the next natural question to ask is whether it also works for list comprehensions—and the answer is *yes*. This support was introduced in PEP 530 (*https://oreil.ly/4qNoH*), and I recommend you take a look at the PEP yourself; it is short and readable. Example 3-27 shows how typical async comprehensions are laid out.

Example 3-27. Async list, dict, and set comprehensions

```
>>> import asyncio
>>>
>>> async def doubler(n):
...     for i in range(n):
...         yield i, i * 2        ❶
...         await asyncio.sleep(0.1)    ❷
...
>>> async def main():
...     result = [x async for x in doubler(3)]        ❸
...     print(result)
...     result = {x: y async for x, y in doubler(3)}    ❹
...     print(result)
...     result = {x async for x in doubler(3)}        ❺
...     print(result)
...
>>> asyncio.run(main())
[(0, 0), (1, 2), (2, 4)]
{0: 0, 1: 2, 2: 4}
{(2, 4), (1, 2), (0, 0)}
```

❶ `doubler()` is a very simple async generator: given an upper value, it'll iterate over a simple range, yielding a tuple of the value and its double.

❷ Sleep a little, just to emphasize that this is really an async function.

❸ An async list comprehension: note how `async for` is used instead of the usual `for`. This difference is the same as that shown in the examples in "Async Iterators: async for" on page 50.

❹ An async dict comprehension; all the usual tricks work, such as unpacking the tuple into x and y so that they can feed the dict comprehension syntax.

❺ The async set comprehension works exactly as you would expect.

You can also use await inside comprehensions, as outlined in PEP 530. This shouldn't be a surprise; await *coro* is a normal expression and can be used in most places you would expect.

It's the async for that makes a comprehension an *async comprehension*, not the presence of await. All that's needed for await to be legal (inside a comprehension) is for it to be used inside the body of a coroutine function—i.e., a function declared with async def. Using await and async for inside the same list comprehension is really combining two separate concepts, but we'll do this anyway in Example 3-28 to make sure you're comfortable with async language syntax.

Example 3-28. Putting it all together

```
>>> import asyncio
>>>
>>> async def f(x):        ❶
...     await asyncio.sleep(0.1)
...     return x + 100
...
>>> async def factory(n):  ❷
...     for x in range(n):
...         await asyncio.sleep(0.1)
...         yield f, x      ❸
...
>>> async def main():
...     results = [await f(x) async for f, x in factory(3)]  ❹
...     print('results = ', results)
...
>>> asyncio.run(main())
results =  [100, 101, 102]
```

❶ A simple coroutine function: sleep for a bit; then return the parameter plus 100.

❷ This is an *async generator*, which we will call inside an async list comprehension a bit farther down, using async for to drive the iteration.

❸ The async generator will yield a tuple of f and the iteration var x. The f return value is a *coroutine function*, not yet a coroutine.

❹ Finally, the async comprehension. This example has been contrived to demonstrate a comprehension that includes *both* async for and await. Let's break down what's happening inside the comprehension. First, the factory(3) call returns an async generator, which must be driven by iteration. Because it's an *async* generator, you can't just use for; you must use async for.

The values produced by the async generator are a tuple of a coroutine function f and an int. Calling the coroutine function f() produces a coroutine, which must be evaluated with await.

Note that inside the comprehension, the use of await has nothing at all to do with the use of async for: they are doing completely different things and acting on different objects entirely.

Starting Up and Shutting Down (Gracefully!)

Most async-based programs are going to be long-running, network-based applications. This domain holds a surprising amount of complexity in dealing with how to start up and shut down correctly.

Of the two, startup is simpler. The standard way of starting up an asyncio application is to have a main() coroutine function and call it with asyncio.run(), as shown in Example 3-2 at the beginning of this chapter.

Generally, startup will be fairly straightforward; for the server case described earlier, you can read more about it in the docs (*http://bit.ly/2FrKaIV*). We'll also briefly look at a demonstration of server startup in an upcoming code example.

Shutdown is much more intricate. For shutdown, I previously covered the dance that happens inside asyncio.run(). When the async def main() function exits, the following actions are taken:

1. Collect all the still-pending task objects (if any).
2. Cancel these tasks (this raises CancelledError inside each running coroutine, which you may choose to handle in a try/except within the body of the coroutine function).
3. Gather all these tasks into a *group* task.
4. Use run_until_complete() on the group task to wait for them to finish—i.e., let the CancelledError exception be raised and dealt with.

asyncio.run() performs these actions for you, but in spite of this assistance, a rite of passage in building your first few nontrivial asyncio apps is going to be trying to get rid of error messages like "Task was destroyed but it is pending!" during shutdown. This happens because your application was not expecting one or more of the preceding steps. Example 3-29 is an example of a script that raises this annoying error.

Example 3-29. Destroyer of pending tasks

```
# taskwarning.py
import asyncio
```

```
async def f(delay):
    await asyncio.sleep(delay)

loop = asyncio.get_event_loop()
t1 = loop.create_task(f(1))  ❶
t2 = loop.create_task(f(2))  ❷
loop.run_until_complete(t1)  ❸
loop.close()
```

❶   Task 1 will run for 1 second.

❷   Task 2 will run for 2 seconds.

❸   Run only until task 1 is complete.

Running it produces the following output:

```
$ python taskwarning.py
Task was destroyed but it is pending!
task: <Task pending coro=<f() done, defined at [...snip...]>
```

This error is telling you that some tasks had not yet been completed when the loop was closed. We want to avoid this, and that is why the idiomatic shutdown procedure is to collect all unfinished tasks, cancel them, and then let them all finish *before* closing the loop. asyncio.run() does all of these steps for you, but it is important to understand the process in detail so that you will be able to handle more complex situations.

Let's look at a more detailed code sample that illustrates all these phases. Example 3-30 is a mini case study with a Telnet-based echo server.

Example 3-30. Asyncio application life cycle (based on the TCP echo server in the Python documentation)

```
# telnetdemo.py
import asyncio
from asyncio import StreamReader, StreamWriter

async def echo(reader: StreamReader, writer: StreamWriter):  ❶
    print('New connection.')
    try:
        while data := await reader.readline():  ❷
            writer.write(data.upper())  ❸
            await writer.drain()
        print('Leaving Connection.')
    except asyncio.CancelledError:  ❹
        print('Connection dropped!')

async def main(host='127.0.0.1', port=8888):
```

```
    server = await asyncio.start_server(echo, host, port) ❺
    async with server:
        await server.serve_forever()

try:
    asyncio.run(main())
except KeyboardInterrupt:
    print('Bye!')
```

❶ This echo() coroutine function will be used (by the server) to create a coroutine
  for each connection made. The function is using the streams API for networking
  with asyncio.

❷ To keep the connection alive, we'll have an infinite loop to wait for messages.

❸ Return the data back to the sender, but in ALL CAPS.

❹ If this task is *cancelled*, we'll print a message.

❺ This code for starting a TCP server is taken directly from the Python 3.8
  documentation.

After starting the echo server, you can telnet to and interact with it:

```
$ telnet 127.0.0.1 8888
Trying 127.0.0.1...
Connected to 127.0.0.1.
Escape character is '^]'.
hi!
HI!
stop shouting
STOP SHOUTING
^]
telnet> q/
Connection closed.
```

The server output for that session looks like this (the server keeps running until we
hit Ctrl-C):

```
$ python telnetdemo.py
New connection.
Leaving Connection.
^CBye!
```

In the Telnet session just shown, the client (i.e., Telnet) closed the connection before
the server was stopped, but let's see what happens if we shut down our server while a
connection is active. We'll see the following output from the server process:

```
$ python telnetdemo.py
New connection.
^CConnection dropped!
Bye!
```

Here you can see that the exception handler for CancelledError was triggered. Now let's imagine that this is a real-world production application, and we want to send all events about dropped connections to a monitoring service. The code sample might be modified to look like Example 3-31.

Example 3-31. Creating a task inside a cancellation handler

```
# telnetdemo.py
import asyncio
from asyncio import StreamReader, StreamWriter

async def send_event(msg: str):    ❶
    await asyncio.sleep(1)

async def echo(reader: StreamReader, writer: StreamWriter):
    print('New connection.')
    try:
        while (data := await reader.readline()):
            writer.write(data.upper())
            await writer.drain()
        print('Leaving Connection.')
    except asyncio.CancelledError:
        msg = 'Connection dropped!'
        print(msg)
        asyncio.create_task(send_event(msg))    ❷

async def main(host='127.0.0.1', port=8888):
    server = await asyncio.start_server(echo, host, port)
    async with server:
        await server.serve_forever()

try:
    asyncio.run(main())
except KeyboardInterrupt:
    print('Bye!')
```

❶ Pretend that this coroutine actually contacts an external server to submit event notifications.

❷ Because the event notifier involves network access, it is common for such calls to be made in a separate async task; that's why we're using the create_task() function here.

This code has a bug, however. It becomes obvious if we rerun the example, and make sure to stop the server (with Ctrl-C) while a connection is active:

```
$ python telnetdemo.py
New connection.
^CConnection dropped!
Bye!
Task was destroyed but it is pending!
task: <Task pending name='Task-6' coro=<send_event() done, ...>
```

To understand why this is happening, we must go back to the sequence of cleanup events that `asyncio.run()` does during the shutdown phase; in particular, the important part is that when we press Ctrl-C, all the currently active tasks are collected and cancelled. At this point, *only those tasks* are then awaited, and `asyncio.run()` returns immediately after that. The bug in our modified code is that we created a *new* task inside the cancellation handler of our existing "echo" task. This new task was created only after `asyncio.run()` had collected and cancelled all the tasks in the process.

This is why it is important to be aware of how `asyncio.run()` works.

As a general rule of thumb, try to avoid creating new tasks inside `CancelledError` exception handlers. If you must, be sure to also `await` the new task or future inside the scope of the same function.

And finally: if you're using a library or framework, make sure to follow its documentation on how you should perform startup and shutdown. Third-party frameworks usually provide their own functions for startup and shutdown, and they'll provide event hooks for customization. You can see an example of these hooks with the Sanic framework in "Case Study: Cache Invalidation" on page 115.

What Is the return_exceptions=True for in gather()?

You may have noticed the keyword argument `return_exceptions=True` in the call to `gather()` in Examples 3-3 and 3-1 during the shutdown sequence, but I very sneakily said nothing about it at the time. `asyncio.run()` also uses `gather()` and `return_exceptions=True` internally, and the time has come for further discussion.

Unfortunately, the default is `gather(..., return_exceptions=False)`. This default is problematic for most situations, including the shutdown process, and this is why `asyncio.run()` sets the parameter to `True`. It's a little complicated to explain directly; instead, let's step through a sequence of observations that'll make it much easier to understand:

1. `run_until_complete()` operates on a future; during shutdown, it's the future returned by `gather()`.

2. If that future raises an exception, the exception will *also* be raised out of `run_until_complete()`, which means that the loop will stop.

3. If `run_until_complete()` is being used on a group future, any exception raised inside *any of the subtasks* will also be raised in the "group" future if it isn't handled in the subtask. Note this includes `CancelledError`.

4. If only some tasks handle `CancelledError` and others don't, the ones that don't will cause the loop to stop. This means that the loop will be stopped *before* all the tasks are done.

5. For shutdown, we really don't want this behavior. We want `run_until_complete()` to finish only when all the tasks in the group have finished, regardless of whether some of the tasks raise exceptions.

6. Hence we have `gather(*, return_exceptions=True)`: that setting makes the "group" future treat exceptions from the subtasks as *returned values*, so that they don't bubble out and interfere with `run_until_complete()`.

And there you have it: the relationship between `return_exceptions=True` and `run_until_complete()`. An undesirable consequence of capturing exceptions in this way is that some errors may escape your attention because they're now (effectively) being handled inside the group task. If this is a concern, you can obtain the output list from `run_until_complete()` and scan it for any subclasses of `Exception`, and then write log messages appropriate for your situation. Example 3-32 demonstrates this approach.

Example 3-32. All the tasks will complete

```
# alltaskscomplete.py
import asyncio

async def f(delay):
    await asyncio.sleep(1 / delay)    ❶
    return delay

loop = asyncio.get_event_loop()
for i in range(10):
    loop.create_task(f(i))
pending = asyncio.all_tasks()
group = asyncio.gather(*pending, return_exceptions=True)
results = loop.run_until_complete(group)
print(f'Results: {results}')
loop.close()
```

① It would be awful if someone were to pass in a zero…

Here's the output:

```
$ python alltaskscomplete.py
Results: [6, 9, 3, 7, ...
         ZeroDivisionError('division by zero',), 4, ...
         8, 1, 5, 2]
```

Without `return_exceptions=True`, the `ZeroDivisionError` would be raised from `run_until_complete()`, stopping the loop and thus preventing the other tasks from finishing.

In the next section, we look at handling signals (beyond KeyboardInterrupt), but before we get there, it's worth keeping in mind that graceful shutdown is one of the more difficult aspects of network programming, and this remains true for `asyncio`. The information in this section is merely a start. I encourage you to have specific tests for clean shutdown in your own automated test suites. Different applications often require different strategies.

 I've published a tiny package on the Python package index (PyPI) called `aiorun` (*https://oreil.ly/kQDt8*), primarily for my own experiments and education in dealing with `asyncio` shutdown, that incorporates many ideas from this section. It may also be useful for you to tinker with the code and experiment with your own ideas around `asyncio` shutdown scenarios.

Signals

Previous examples showed how the event loop is stopped with a `KeyboardInterrupt`; i.e., pressing Ctrl-C. Internally within `asyncio.run()`, the raised `KeyboardInterrupt` effectively unblocks a `loop.run_until_complete()` call and allows the subsequent shutdown sequence to happen.

`KeyboardInterrupt` corresponds to the `SIGINT` signal. In network services, the more common signal for process termination is actually `SIGTERM`, and this is also the default signal when you use the `kill` command in a Unix shell.

The `kill` command on Unix systems is deceptively named: all it does it send signals to a process. Without arguments, `kill <PID>` will send a `TERM` signal: your process can receive the signal and do a graceful shutdown, or simply ignore it! That's a bad idea, though, because if your process doesn't stop eventually, the next thing the would-be killer usually does is `kill -s KILL <PID>`, which sends the `KILL` signal. This will shut you down, and there's nothing your program can do about it. Receiving the `TERM` (or `INT`) signal is your opportunity to shut down in a controlled way.

`asyncio` has built-in support for handling process signals, but there's a surprising degree of complexity around signal handling in general (not specific to `asyncio`). We cannot cover everything here, but we can have a look at some of the more basic considerations that need to be made. Example 3-33 will produce the following output:

```
$ python shell_signal01.py
<Your app is running>
<Your app is running>
<Your app is running>
<Your app is running>
^CGot signal: SIGINT, shutting down.
```

I pressed Ctrl-C to stop the program, as shown on the last line. Example 3-33 intentionally avoids using the convenient `asyncio.run()` function because I want to warn you about specific traps in handling the two most common signals, `SIGTERM` and `SIGINT`, during your shutdown sequence. After we discuss these, I will show a final example of signal handling using the more convenient `asyncio.run()` function.

Example 3-33. Refresher for using KeyboardInterrupt as a SIGINT handler

```
# shell_signal01.py
import asyncio

async def main():    ❶
    while True:
        print('<Your app is running>')
        await asyncio.sleep(1)


if __name__ == '__main__':
    loop = asyncio.get_event_loop()
    task = loop.create_task(main())    ❷
    try:
        loop.run_until_complete(task)
    except KeyboardInterrupt:    ❸
        print('Got signal: SIGINT, shutting down.')
    tasks = asyncio.all_tasks(loop=loop)
    for t in tasks:
```

```
            t.cancel()
    group = asyncio.gather(*tasks, return_exceptions=True)
    loop.run_until_complete(group)
    loop.close()
```

❶ This is the main part of our application. To keep things simple, we're just going to sleep in an infinite loop.

❷ This startup and shutdown sequence will be familiar to you from the previous section. We schedule `main()`, call `run_forever()`, and wait for something to stop the loop.

❸ In this case, only Ctrl-C will stop the loop. Then we handle `KeyboardInterrupt` and do all the necessary cleanup bits, as covered in the previous sections.

So far, that's pretty straightforward. Now I'm going to complicate things. Suppose that:

- One of your colleagues asks that you please handle `SIGTERM` in addition to `SIGINT` as a shutdown signal.

- In your real application, you need to do cleanup inside your `main()` coroutine; you will need to handle `CancelledError`, and the cleanup code inside the exception handler will take several seconds to finish (imagine that you have to communicate with network peers and close a bunch of socket connections).

- Your app must not do weird things if you're sent signals multiple times (such as rerunning any shutdown steps); after you receive the first shutdown signal, you want to simply ignore any new signals until exit.

`asyncio` provides enough granularity in the API to handle all these situations. Example 3-34 modifies the previous simple code example to include these new features.

Example 3-34. Handle both SIGINT and SIGTERM, but stop the loop only once

```
# shell_signal02.py
import asyncio
from signal import SIGINT, SIGTERM    ❶

async def main():
    try:
        while True:
            print('<Your app is running>')
            await asyncio.sleep(1)
    except asyncio.CancelledError:     ❷
        for i in range(3):
```

```
            print('<Your app is shutting down...>')
            await asyncio.sleep(1)
    def handler(sig):    ❸
        loop.stop()    ❹
        print(f'Got signal: {sig!s}, shutting down.')
        loop.remove_signal_handler(SIGTERM)    ❺
        loop.add_signal_handler(SIGINT, lambda: None)    ❻

    if __name__ == '__main__':
        loop = asyncio.get_event_loop()
        for sig in (SIGTERM, SIGINT):    ❼
            loop.add_signal_handler(sig, handler, sig)
        loop.create_task(main())
        loop.run_forever()    ❽
        tasks = asyncio.all_tasks(loop=loop)
        for t in tasks:
            t.cancel()
        group = asyncio.gather(*tasks, return_exceptions=True)
        loop.run_until_complete(group)
        loop.close()
```

❶ Import the signal values from the standard library `signal` module.

❷ This time, our `main()` coroutine is going to do some cleanup internally. When the cancellation signal is received (initiated by cancelling each of the tasks), there will be a period of 3 seconds where `main()` will continue running during the `run_until_complete()` phase of the shutdown process. It'll print, "Your app is shutting down…".

❸ This is a callback handler for when we receive a signal. It is configured on the loop via the call to `add_signal_handler()` a bit farther down.

❹ The primary purpose of the handler is to stop the loop: this will unblock the `loop.run_forever()` call and allow pending task collection and cancellation, and the `run_complete()` for shutdown.

❺ Since we are now in shutdown mode, we *don't want* another SIGINT or SIGTERM to trigger this handler again: that would call `loop.stop()` during the `run_until_complete()` phase, which would interfere with our shutdown process. Therefore, we *remove* the signal handler for SIGTERM from the loop.

❻ This is a "gotcha": we can't simply remove the handler for SIGINT, because if we did that, KeyboardInterrupt would again become the handler for SIGINT, the same as it was before we added our own handlers. Instead, we set an empty lambda function as the handler. This means that KeyboardInterrupt stays away, and SIGINT (and Ctrl-C) has no effect.[10]

❼ Here the signal handlers are attached to the loop. Note that, as discussed previously, setting a handler on SIGINT means a KeyboardInterrupt will no longer be raised on SIGINT. The raising of a KeyboardInterrupt is the "default" handler for SIGINT and is preconfigured in Python until you do something to change the handler, as we're doing here.

❽ As usual, execution blocks on run_forever() until something stops the loop. In this case, the loop will be stopped inside handler() if either SIGINT or SIGTERM is sent to our process. The remainder of the code is the same as before.

Here's the output:

```
$ python shell_signal02.py
<Your app is running>
<Your app is running>
<Your app is running>
<Your app is running>
<Your app is running>
^CGot signal: Signals.SIGINT, shutting down.
<Your app is shutting down...>
^C<Your app is shutting down...>  ❶
^C<Your app is shutting down...>
```

❶ I hit Ctrl-C a bunch of times during the shutdown phase, but as expected, nothing happened until the main() coroutine eventually completed.

In these examples, I've controlled the life cycle of the event loop the hard way, but this was necessary to explain the components of the shutdown procedure. In practice, we would much prefer to use the more convenient asyncio.run() function. Example 3-35 retains the features of the preceding signal-handling design, but also takes advantage of the convenience of asyncio.run().

Example 3-35. Signal handling when using asyncio.run()

```
# shell_signal02b.py
import asyncio
from signal import SIGINT, SIGTERM

async def main():
```

---

10 add_signal_handler() should probably be named set_signal_handler(), since you can have only one handler per signal type; calling add_signal_handler() a second time for the same signal will replace the existing handler for that signal.

```
    loop = asyncio.get_running_loop()
    for sig in (SIGTERM, SIGINT):
        loop.add_signal_handler(sig, handler, sig)   ❶

    try:
        while True:
            print('<Your app is running>')
            await asyncio.sleep(1)
    except asyncio.CancelledError:
        for i in range(3):
            print('<Your app is shutting down...>')
            await asyncio.sleep(1)

def handler(sig):
    loop = asyncio.get_running_loop()
    for task in asyncio.all_tasks(loop=loop):   ❷
        task.cancel()
    print(f'Got signal: {sig!s}, shutting down.')
    loop.remove_signal_handler(SIGTERM)
    loop.add_signal_handler(SIGINT, lambda: None)

if __name__ == '__main__':
    asyncio.run(main())
```

❶ Because `asyncio.run()` takes control of the event loop startup, our first opportunity to change signal handling behavior will be in the `main()` function.

❷ Inside the signal handler, we can't stop the loop as in previous examples, because we'll get warnings about how the loop was stopped before the task created for `main()` was completed. Instead, we can initiate task cancellation here, which will ultimately result in the `main()` task exiting; when that happens, the cleanup handling inside `asyncio.run()` will take over.

Waiting for the Executor During Shutdown

"Quickstart" on page 22 introduced the basic executor interface with Example 3-3, where I pointed out that the blocking `time.sleep()` call was conveniently shorter than the `asyncio.sleep()` call—luckily for us, because it means the executor task completes sooner than the `main()` coroutine, and as a result the program shuts down correctly.

This section examines what happens during shutdown when executor jobs take longer to finish than all the pending `Task` instances. The short answer is: without intervention, you're going to get errors like those produced by the code in Example 3-36.

Example 3-36. The executor takes too long to finish

```python
# quickstart.py
import time
import asyncio

async def main():
    loop = asyncio.get_running_loop()
    loop.run_in_executor(None, blocking)
    print(f'{time.ctime()} Hello!')
    await asyncio.sleep(1.0)
    print(f'{time.ctime()} Goodbye!')

def blocking():
    time.sleep(1.5)  ❶
    print(f"{time.ctime()} Hello from a thread!")

asyncio.run(main())
```

❶ This code sample is exactly the same as the one in Example 3-3, *except* that the sleep time in the blocking function is now longer than in the async one.

Running this code produces the following output:

```
$ python quickstart.py
Fri Jan 24 16:25:08 2020 Hello!
Fri Jan 24 16:25:09 2020 Goodbye!
exception calling callback for <Future at [...snip...]>
Traceback (most recent call last):

<big nasty traceback>

RuntimeError: Event loop is closed
Fri Jan 24 16:25:09 2020 Hello from a thread!
```

What's happening here is that behind the scenes, run_in_executor() does *not* create a Task instance: it returns a Future. That means it isn't included in the set of "active tasks" that get cancelled inside asyncio.run(), and therefore run_until_complete() (called inside asyncio.run()) does *not* wait for the executor task to finish. The RuntimeError is being raised from the internal loop.close() call made inside asyncio.run().

At the time of writing, loop.close() in Python 3.8 does not wait for all executor jobs to finish, and this is why the Future returned from run_in_executor() complains: by the time it resolves, the loop has already been closed. There are discussions about how to improve this in the core Python dev team, but until a solution has been settled on, you're going to need a strategy for handling these errors.

In Python 3.9, the asyncio.run() function has been improved (*https://oreil.ly/ZrpRb*) to correctly wait for executor shutdown, but at the time of writing, this has not yet been backported to Python 3.8.

Several ideas for fixing this spring to mind, all with different trade-offs, and we're going to look at a few of them. My real goal for this exercise is to help you think about the event loop life cycle from different points of view, considering the lifetime management of all the coroutines, threads, and subprocesses that might be interoperating in a nontrivial program.

The first idea—and the easiest to implement, as shown in Example 3-37— is to always await an executor task from inside a coroutine.

Example 3-37. Option A: wrap the executor call inside a coroutine

```
# quickstart.py
import time
import asyncio
from concurrent.futures import ThreadPoolExecutor as Executor

async def main():
    loop = asyncio.get_running_loop()
    future = loop.run_in_executor(None, blocking)    ❶
    try:
        print(f'{time.ctime()} Hello!')
        await asyncio.sleep(1.0)
        print(f'{time.ctime()} Goodbye!')
    finally:
        await future    ❷

def blocking():
    time.sleep(2.0)
    print(f"{time.ctime()} Hello from a thread!")

try:
    asyncio.run(main())
except KeyboardInterrupt:
    print('Bye!')
```

❶ The idea aims at fixing the shortcoming that run_in_executor() returns only a Future instance and not a task. We can't capture the job in all_tasks() (used within asyncio.run()), but we *can* use await on the future. The first part of the plan is to create a future inside the main() function.

❷ We can use the try/finally structure to ensure that we wait for the future to be finished before the main() function returns.

The code works, but it places a heavy limitation on lifetime management of the executor function: it implies that you must use a `try/finally` within every single scope where an executor job is created. We would prefer to spawn executor jobs in the same way that we create async tasks, and still have the shutdown handling inside `asyncio.run()` perform a graceful exit.

The next idea, shown in Example 3-38, is a little more cunning. Since our problem is that an executor creates a future instead of a task, and the shutdown handling inside `asyncio.run()` deals with tasks, our next plan is to wrap the future (produced by the executor) inside a new task object.

Example 3-38. Option B: add the executor future to the gathered tasks

```python
# quickstart.py
import time
import asyncio
from concurrent.futures import ThreadPoolExecutor as Executor

async def make_coro(future):   ❷
    try:
        return await future
    except asyncio.CancelledError:
        return await future

async def main():
    loop = asyncio.get_running_loop()
    future = loop.run_in_executor(None, blocking)
    asyncio.create_task(make_coro(future))   ❶
    print(f'{time.ctime()} Hello!')
    await asyncio.sleep(1.0)
    print(f'{time.ctime()} Goodbye!')

def blocking():
    time.sleep(2.0)
    print(f"{time.ctime()} Hello from a thread!")

try:
    asyncio.run(main())
except KeyboardInterrupt:
    print('Bye!')
```

❶ We take the future returned from the `run_in_executor()` call and pass it into a new utility function, `make_coro()`. The important point here is that we're using `create_task()`, which means that this task *will* appear in the list of `all_tasks()` within the shutdown handling of `asyncio.run()`, and will receive a cancellation during the shutdown process.

❷ This utility function make_coro() simply waits for the future to complete—but crucially, it *continues to wait* for the future even inside the exception handler for CancelledError.

This solution is better behaved during shutdown, and I encourage you to run the example and hit Ctrl-C immediately after "Hello!" is printed. The shutdown process will still wait for make_coro() to exit, which means that it also waits for our executor job to exit. However, this code is very clumsy because you have to wrap every executor Future instance inside a make_coro() call.

If we're willing to give up the convenience of the asyncio.run() function (until Python 3.9 is available), we can do better with custom loop handling, shown in Example 3-39.

Example 3-39. Option C: just like camping, bring your own loop and your own executor

```python
# quickstart.py
import time
import asyncio
from concurrent.futures import ThreadPoolExecutor as Executor

async def main():
    print(f'{time.ctime()} Hello!')
    await asyncio.sleep(1.0)
    print(f'{time.ctime()} Goodbye!')
    loop.stop()

def blocking():
    time.sleep(2.0)
    print(f"{time.ctime()} Hello from a thread!")

loop = asyncio.get_event_loop()
executor = Executor()                               ❶
loop.set_default_executor(executor)                 ❷
loop.create_task(main())
future = loop.run_in_executor(None, blocking)       ❸
try:
    loop.run_forever()
except KeyboardInterrupt:
    print('Cancelled')
tasks = asyncio.all_tasks(loop=loop)
for t in tasks:
    t.cancel()
group = asyncio.gather(*tasks, return_exceptions=True)
loop.run_until_complete(group)
executor.shutdown(wait=True)                        ❹
loop.close()
```

❶ This time, we create our own executor instance.

❷ We have to set our custom executor as the default one for the loop. This means that anywhere the code calls `run_in_executor()`, it'll be using our custom instance.

❸ As before, we run the blocking function.

❹ Finally, we can explicitly wait for all the executor jobs to finish before closing the loop. This will avoid the "Event loop is closed" messages that we saw before. We can do this because we have access to the executor object; the default executor is not exposed in the `asyncio` API, which is why we cannot call `shutdown()` on it and were forced to create our own executor instance.

Finally, we have a strategy with general applicability: you can call `run_in_executor()` anywhere, and your program will still shut down cleanly, even if executor jobs are still running after all the async tasks have completed.

I strongly urge you to experiment with the code examples shown here and try different strategies to create tasks and executor jobs, staggering them in time and trying to shut down cleanly. I expect that a future version of Python will allow the `asyncio.run()` function to wait (internally) for executor jobs to finish, but I hope that the discussion in this section is still useful for you to develop your thinking around clean shutdown handling.

## CHAPTER 4

20 Asyncio Libraries You Aren't Using (But...Oh, Never Mind)

In this chapter, we look at case studies using the new Python features for async programming. We'll be making use of several third-party libraries, as you will in your own projects.

The title of this chapter is a play on the title of a previous book I wrote called *20 Python Libraries You Aren't Using (But Should)* (*https://oreil.ly/HLsvb*) (O'Reilly). Many of those libraries will also be useful in your asyncio-based applications, but this chapter focuses on libraries that have been designed specifically for the new async features in Python.

It is difficult to present asyncio-based code in short snippets. As you have seen in all the previous code samples in the book, I've tried to make each example a complete, runnable program, because application lifetime management is a core consideration for using async programming correctly.

For this reason, most of the case studies in this chapter will be somewhat larger, in terms of lines of code, than is usual for such a book. My goal in using this approach is to make the case studies more useful by giving you a "whole view" of an async program rather than leaving you to figure out how detached fragments might fit together.

 Some of the code samples in this chapter compromise on style in order to save space. I like PEP8 as much as the next Pythonista, but practicality beats purity!

Streams (Standard Library)

Before looking at third-party libraries, let's begin with the standard library. The streams API (*https://oreil.ly/mnMZD*) is the high-level interface offered for async socket programming, and as the following case study will show, it's pretty easy to use. However, application design remains complex simply because of the nature of the domain.

The following case study shows an implementation of a message broker, with an initial naive design followed by a more considered design. Neither should be considered production-ready; my goal is to help you think about the various aspects of concurrent network programming that need to be taken into account when designing such applications.

Case Study: A Message Queue

A *message queue service* is a backend application that receives connections from other applications and passes messages between those connected services, often referred to as *publishers* and *subscribers*. Subscribers typically listen to specific channels for messages, and usually it is possible to configure the message distribution in different channels in two ways: messages can be distributed to all subscribers on a channel (*pub-sub*), or a different message can go to each subscriber one at a time (*point-to-point*).

Recently, I worked on a project that involved using ActiveMQ (*https://oreil.ly/yiaK0*) as a message broker for microservices intercommunication. At a basic level, such a broker (server):

- Maintains persistent socket connections to multiple clients
- Receives messages from clients with a target *channel name*
- Delivers those messages to all *other* clients subscribed to that same channel name

I recall wondering how hard it might be to create such an application. As an added touch, ActiveMQ can perform both models of message distribution, and the two models are generally differentiated by the channel name:

- Channel names with the prefix `/topic` (e.g., `/topic/customer/registration`) are managed with the pub-sub (*https://oreil.ly/y6cYr*) pattern, where all channel subscribers get all messages.
- Channel names with the prefix `/queue` are handled with the point-to-point (*http://bit.ly/2CeNbxr*) model, in which messages on a channel are distributed between channel subscribers in a round-robin fashion: each subscriber gets a unique message.

In our case study, we will build a toy message broker with these basic features. The first issue we must address is that TCP is not a message-based protocol: we just get streams of bytes on the wire. We need to create our own protocol for the structure of messages, and the simplest protocol is to prefix each message with a size header, followed by a message payload of that size. The utility library in Example 4-1 provides *read* and *write* capabilities for such messages.

Example 4-1. Message protocol: read and write

```
# msgproto.py
from asyncio import StreamReader, StreamWriter

async def read_msg(stream: StreamReader) -> bytes:
    size_bytes = await stream.readexactly(4)       ❶
    size = int.from_bytes(size_bytes, byteorder='big')   ❷
    data = await stream.readexactly(size)          ❸
    return data

async def send_msg(stream: StreamWriter, data: bytes):
    size_bytes = len(data).to_bytes(4, byteorder='big')
    stream.writelines([size_bytes, data])          ❹
    await stream.drain()
```

❶ Get the first 4 bytes. This is the size prefix.

❷ Those 4 bytes must be converted into an integer.

❸ Now we know the payload size, so we read that off the stream.

❹ *Write* is the inverse of *read*: first we send the length of the data, encoded as 4 bytes, and thereafter the data.

Now that we have a rudimentary message protocol, we can focus on the message broker application in Example 4-2.

Example 4-2. A 40-line prototype server

```
# mq_server.py
import asyncio
from asyncio import StreamReader, StreamWriter, gather
from collections import deque, defaultdict
from typing import Deque, DefaultDict
from msgproto import read_msg, send_msg          ❶

SUBSCRIBERS: DefaultDict[bytes, Deque] = defaultdict(deque)   ❷

async def client(reader: StreamReader, writer: StreamWriter):
    peername = writer.get_extra_info('peername')   ❸
```

```
    subscribe_chan = await read_msg(reader)  ❹
    SUBSCRIBERS[subscribe_chan].append(writer)  ❺
    print(f'Remote {peername} subscribed to {subscribe_chan}')
    try:
      while channel_name := await read_msg(reader):  ❻
        data = await read_msg(reader)  ❼
        print(f'Sending to {channel_name}: {data[:19]}...')
        conns = SUBSCRIBERS[channel_name]  ❽
        if conns and channel_name.startswith(b'/queue'):  ❾
          conns.rotate()  ❿
          conns = [conns[0]]  ⓫
        await gather(*[send_msg(c, data) for c in conns])  ⓬
    except asyncio.CancelledError:
      print(f'Remote {peername} closing connection.')
      writer.close()
      await writer.wait_closed()
    except asyncio.IncompleteReadError:
      print(f'Remote {peername} disconnected')
    finally:
      print(f'Remote {peername} closed')
      SUBSCRIBERS[subscribe_chan].remove(writer)  ⓭

async def main(*args, **kwargs):
    server = await asyncio.start_server(*args, **kwargs)
    async with server:
        await server.serve_forever()

try:
    asyncio.run(main(client, host='127.0.0.1', port=25000))
except KeyboardInterrupt:
    print('Bye!')
```

❶ Imports from our *msgproto.py* module.

❷ A global collection of currently active subscribers. Every time a client connects, they must first send a channel name they're subscribing to. A deque will hold all the subscribers for a particular channel.

❸ The client() coroutine function will produce a long-lived coroutine for each new connection. Think of it as a callback for the TCP server started in main(). On this line, I've shown how the host and port of the remote peer can be obtained, for example, for logging.

❹ Our protocol for clients is the following:

  - On first connect, a client *must* send a message containing the channel to subscribe to (here, subscribe_chan).

  - Thereafter, for the life of the connection, a client sends a message to a channel by first sending a message containing the destination channel name, followed by a message containing the data. Our broker will send such data messages to every client subscribed to that channel name.

❺ Add the `StreamWriter` instance to the global collection of subscribers.

❻ An infinite loop, waiting for data from this client. The first message from a client must be the destination channel name.

❼ Next comes the actual data to distribute to the channel.

❽ Get the deque of subscribers on the target channel.

❾ Some special handling if the channel name begins with the magic word `/queue`: in this case, we send the data to *only one* of the subscribers, not all of them. This can be used for sharing work between a bunch of workers, rather than the usual pub-sub notification scheme, where all subscribers on a channel get all the messages.

❿ Here is why we use a deque and not a list: rotation of the deque is how we keep track of which client is next in line for `/queue` distribution. This seems expensive until you realize that a single deque rotation is an O(1) operation.

⓫ Target only whichever client is first; this changes after every rotation.

⓬ Create a list of coroutines for sending the message to each writer, and then unpack these into `gather()` so we can wait for all of the sending to complete.

This line is a bad flaw in our program, but it may not be obvious why: though it may be true that all of the sending to each subscriber will happen concurrently, what happens if we have one very slow client? In this case, the `gather()` will finish only when the slowest subscriber has received its data. We can't receive any more data from the sending client until all these `send_msg()` coroutines finish. This slows all message distribution to the speed of the slowest subscriber.

⓭ When leaving the `client()` coroutine, we make sure to remove ourselves from the global `SUBSCRIBERS` collection. Unfortunately, this is an O(n) operation, which can be a little expensive for very large n. A different data structure would fix this, but for now we console ourselves with the knowledge that connections are intended to be long-lived—thus, there should be few disconnection events— and n is unlikely to be very large (say ~10,000 as a rough order-of-magnitude estimate), and this code is at least easy to understand.

So that's our server; now we need clients, and then we can show some output. For demonstration purposes, I'll make two kinds of clients: a *sender* and a *listener*. The server doesn't differentiate; all clients are the same. The distinction between sender and listener behavior is only for educational purposes. Example 4-3 shows the code for the listener application.

Example 4-3. Listener: a toolkit for listening for messages on our message broker

```
# mq_client_listen.py
import asyncio
import argparse, uuid
from msgproto import read_msg, send_msg

async def main(args):
  me = uuid.uuid4().hex[:8]  ❶
  print(f'Starting up {me}')
  reader, writer = await asyncio.open_connection(
    args.host, args.port)  ❷
  print(f'I am {writer.get_extra_info("sockname")}')
  channel = args.listen.encode()  ❸
  await send_msg(writer, channel)  ❹
  try:
    while data := await read_msg(reader):  ❺
      print(f'Received by {me}: {data[:20]}')
    print('Connection ended.')
  except asyncio.IncompleteReadError:
    print('Server closed.')
  finally:
    writer.close()
    await writer.wait_closed()


if __name__ == '__main__':
  parser = argparse.ArgumentParser()  ❻
  parser.add_argument('--host', default='localhost')
  parser.add_argument('--port', default=25000)
  parser.add_argument('--listen', default='/topic/foo')
  try:
    asyncio.run(main(parser.parse_args()))
  except KeyboardInterrupt:
    print('Bye!')
```

❶ The uuid standard library module is a convenient way of creating an "identity" for this listener. If you start up multiple instances, each will have its own identity, and you'll be able to track what is happening in the logs.

❷ Open a connection to the server.

❸ The channel to subscribe to is an input parameter, captured in `args.listen`. Encode it into bytes before sending.

❹ By our protocol rules (as discussed in the broker code analysis previously), the first thing to do after connecting is to send the channel name to subscribe to.

❺ This loop does nothing else but wait for data to appear on the socket.

❻ The command-line arguments for this program make it easy to point to a host, a port, and a channel name to listen to.

The code for the other client, the sender program shown in Example 4-4, is similar in structure to the listener module.

Example 4-4. Sender: a toolkit for sending data to our message broker

```python
# mq_client_sender.py
import asyncio
import argparse, uuid
from itertools import count
from msgproto import send_msg

async def main(args):
    me = uuid.uuid4().hex[:8]    ❶
    print(f'Starting up {me}')
    reader, writer = await asyncio.open_connection(
        host=args.host, port=args.port)    ❷
    print(f'I am {writer.get_extra_info("sockname")}')

    channel = b'/null'    ❸
    await send_msg(writer, channel)    ❹

    chan = args.channel.encode()    ❺
    try:
        for i in count():    ❻
            await asyncio.sleep(args.interval)    ❼
            data = b'X'*args.size or f'Msg {i} from {me}'.encode()
            try:
                await send_msg(writer, chan)
                await send_msg(writer, data)    ❽
            except OSError:
                print('Connection ended.')
                break
    except asyncio.CancelledError:
        writer.close()
        await writer.wait_closed()

if __name__ == '__main__':
    parser = argparse.ArgumentParser()    ❾
```

```
parser.add_argument('--host', default='localhost')
parser.add_argument('--port', default=25000, type=int)
parser.add_argument('--channel', default='/topic/foo')
parser.add_argument('--interval', default=1, type=float)
parser.add_argument('--size', default=0, type=int)
try:
    asyncio.run(main(parser.parse_args()))
except KeyboardInterrupt:
    print('Bye!')
```

❶ As with the listener, claim an identity.

❷ Reach out and make a connection.

❸ According to our protocol rules, the first thing to do after connecting to the
server is to give the name of the channel to subscribe to; however, since we are a
sender, we don't really care about subscribing to any channels. Nevertheless, the
protocol requires it, so just provide a null channel to subscribe to (we won't
actually listen for anything).

❹ Send the channel to subscribe to.

❺ The command-line parameter `args.channel` provides the channel *to which* we
want to send messages. It must be converted to bytes first before sending.

❻ Using `itertools.count()` is like a `while True` loop, except that we get an iteration variable to use. We use this in the debugging messages since it makes it a bit
easier to track which message got sent from where.

❼ The delay between sent messages is an input parameter, `args.interval`. The next
line generates the message payload. It's either a bytestring of specified size
(`args.size`) or a descriptive message. This flexibility is just for testing.

❽ Note that *two* messages are sent here: the first is the destination channel name,
and the second is the payload.

❾ As with the listener, there are a bunch of command-line options for tweaking the
sender: `channel` determines the target channel to send to, while `interval` controls the delay between sends. The `size` parameter controls the size of each message payload.

We now have a broker, a listener, and a sender; it's time to see some output. To produce the following code snippets, I started up the server, then two listeners, and then
a sender. Then, after a few messages had been sent, I stopped the server with Ctrl-C.

The server output is shown in Example 4-5, the sender output in Example 4-6, and the listener output in Examples 4-7 and 4-8.

Example 4-5. Message broker (server) output

```
$ mq_server.py
Remote ('127.0.0.1', 55382) subscribed to b'/queue/blah'
Remote ('127.0.0.1', 55386) subscribed to b'/queue/blah'
Remote ('127.0.0.1', 55390) subscribed to b'/null'
Sending to b'/queue/blah': b'Msg 0 from 6b5a8e1d'...
Sending to b'/queue/blah': b'Msg 1 from 6b5a8e1d'...
Sending to b'/queue/blah': b'Msg 2 from 6b5a8e1d'...
Sending to b'/queue/blah': b'Msg 3 from 6b5a8e1d'...
Sending to b'/queue/blah': b'Msg 4 from 6b5a8e1d'...
Sending to b'/queue/blah': b'Msg 5 from 6b5a8e1d'...
^CBye!
Remote ('127.0.0.1', 55382) closing connection.
Remote ('127.0.0.1', 55382) closed
Remote ('127.0.0.1', 55390) closing connection.
Remote ('127.0.0.1', 55390) closed
Remote ('127.0.0.1', 55386) closing connection.
Remote ('127.0.0.1', 55386) closed
```

Example 4-6. Sender (client) output

```
$ mq_client_sender.py --channel /queue/blah
Starting up 6b5a8e1d
I am ('127.0.0.1', 55390)
Connection ended.
```

Example 4-7. Listener 1 (client) output

```
$ mq_client_listen.py --listen /queue/blah
Starting up 9ae04690
I am ('127.0.0.1', 55382)
Received by 9ae04690: b'Msg 1 from 6b5a8e1d'
Received by 9ae04690: b'Msg 3 from 6b5a8e1d'
Received by 9ae04690: b'Msg 5 from 6b5a8e1d'
Server closed.
```

Example 4-8. Listener 2 (client) output

```
$ mq_client_listen.py --listen /queue/blah
Starting up bd4e3baa
I am ('127.0.0.1', 55386)
Received by bd4e3baa: b'Msg 0 from 6b5a8e1d'
Received by bd4e3baa: b'Msg 2 from 6b5a8e1d'
Received by bd4e3baa: b'Msg 4 from 6b5a8e1d'
Server closed.
```

Our toy message broker works. The code is also pretty easy to understand, given such a complex problem domain, but unfortunately, the design of the broker code itself is problematic.

The problem is that, for a particular client, we send messages to subscribers in the same coroutine as where new messages are received. This means that if any subscriber is slow to consume what we're sending, it might take a long time for that await gather(...) line in Example 4-2 to complete, and we cannot receive and process more messages while we wait.

Instead, we need to decouple the receiving of messages from the sending of messages. In the next case study, we refactor our code to do exactly that.

Case Study: Improving the Message Queue

In this case study, we improve the design of our toy message broker. The listener and sender programs remain as is. The specific improvement in the new broker design is to decouple sending and receiving messages; this will resolve the problem where a slow subscriber would also slow down receiving new messages, as discussed in the previous section. The new code, shown in Example 4-9, is a bit longer but not terribly so.

Example 4-9. Message broker: improved design

```
# mq_server_plus.py
import asyncio
from asyncio import StreamReader, StreamWriter, Queue
from collections import deque, defaultdict
from contextlib import suppress
from typing import Deque, DefaultDict, Dict
from msgproto import read_msg, send_msg

SUBSCRIBERS: DefaultDict[bytes, Deque] = defaultdict(deque)
SEND_QUEUES: DefaultDict[StreamWriter, Queue] = defaultdict(Queue)
CHAN_QUEUES: Dict[bytes, Queue] = {}  ❶

async def client(reader: StreamReader, writer: StreamWriter):
  peername = writer.get_extra_info('peername')
  subscribe_chan = await read_msg(reader)
  SUBSCRIBERS[subscribe_chan].append(writer)  ❷
  send_task = asyncio.create_task(
      send_client(writer, SEND_QUEUES[writer]))  ❸
  print(f'Remote {peername} subscribed to {subscribe_chan}')
  try:
    while channel_name := await read_msg(reader):
      data = await read_msg(reader)
      if channel_name not in CHAN_QUEUES:  ❹
        CHAN_QUEUES[channel_name] = Queue(maxsize=10)  ❺
```

```
            asyncio.create_task(chan_sender(channel_name))  ❻
        await CHAN_QUEUES[channel_name].put(data)  ❼
    except asyncio.CancelledError:
      print(f'Remote {peername} connection cancelled.')
    except asyncio.IncompleteReadError:
      print(f'Remote {peername} disconnected')
    finally:
      print(f'Remote {peername} closed')
      await SEND_QUEUES[writer].put(None)  ❽
      await send_task  ❾
      del SEND_QUEUES[writer]  ❿
      SUBSCRIBERS[subscribe_chan].remove(writer)

async def send_client(writer: StreamWriter, queue: Queue):  ⓫
    while True:
        try:
            data = await queue.get()
        except asyncio.CancelledError:
            continue

        if not data:
            break

        try:
            await send_msg(writer, data)
        except asyncio.CancelledError:
            await send_msg(writer, data)

    writer.close()
    await writer.wait_closed()

async def chan_sender(name: bytes):
    with suppress(asyncio.CancelledError):
        while True:
            writers = SUBSCRIBERS[name]
            if not writers:
                await asyncio.sleep(1)
                continue  ⓬
            if name.startswith(b'/queue'):  ⓭
                writers.rotate()
                writers = [writers[0]]
            if not (msg := await CHAN_QUEUES[name].get()):  ⓮
                break
            for writer in writers:
                if not SEND_QUEUES[writer].full():
                    print(f'Sending to {name}: {msg[:19]}...')
                    await SEND_QUEUES[writer].put(msg)  ⓯

async def main(*args, **kwargs):
    server = await asyncio.start_server(*args, **kwargs)
    async with server:
        await server.serve_forever()
```

```
try:
    asyncio.run(main(client, host='127.0.0.1', port=25000))
except KeyboardInterrupt:
    print('Bye!')
```

❶ In the previous implementation, there were only SUBSCRIBERS; now there are SEND_QUEUES and CHAN_QUEUES as global collections. This is a consequence of completely decoupling the *receiving* and *sending* of data. SEND_QUEUES has one queue entry for each client connection: all data that must be sent to that client must be placed onto that queue. (If you peek ahead, the send_client() coroutine will pull data off SEND_QUEUES and send it.)

❷ Up until this point in the client() coroutine function, the code is the same as in the simple server: the subscribed channel name is received, and we add the StreamWriter instance for the new client to the global SUBSCRIBERS collection.

❸ This is new: we create a long-lived task that will do all the sending of data to this client. The task will run independently as a separate coroutine and will pull messages off the supplied queue, SEND_QUEUES[writer], for sending.

❹ Now we're inside the loop where we receive data. Remember that we always receive two messages: one for the destination channel name, and one for the data. We're going to create a new, dedicated Queue for every destination channel, and that's what CHAN_QUEUES is for: when any client wants to push data to a channel, we're going to put that data onto the appropriate queue and then go immediately back to listening for more data. This approach decouples the distribution of messages from the receiving of messages from this client.

❺ If there isn't already a queue for the target channel, make one.

❻ Create a dedicated and long-lived task for that channel. The coroutine chan_sender() will be responsible for taking data off the channel queue and distributing that data to subscribers.

❼ Place the newly received data onto the specific channel's queue. If the queue fills up, we'll wait here until there is space for the new data. Waiting here means we won't be reading any new data off the socket, which means that the client will have to wait on sending new data into the socket on its side. This isn't necessarily a bad thing, since it communicates so-called *back-pressure* to this client. (Alternatively, you could choose to drop messages here if the use case is OK with that.)

❽ When the connection is closed, it's time to clean up. The long-lived task we created for sending data to this client, send_task, can be shut down by placing None onto its queue, SEND_QUEUES[writer] (check the code for send_client()). It's important to use a value on the queue, rather than outright cancellation, because there may already be data on that queue and we want that data to be sent out before send_client() is ended.

❾ Wait for that sender task to finish…

❿ …then remove the entry in the SEND_QUEUES collection (and in the next line, we also remove the sock from the SUBSCRIBERS collection as before).

⓫ The send_client() coroutine function is very nearly a textbook example of pulling work off a queue. Note how the coroutine will exit only if None is placed onto the queue. Note also how we suppress CancelledError *inside* the loop: this is because we want this task to be closed only by receiving a None on the queue. This way, all pending data on the queue can be sent out before shutdown.

⓬ chan_sender() is the distribution logic for a channel: it sends data from a dedicated channel Queue instance to all the subscribers on that channel. But what happens if there are no subscribers for this channel yet? We'll just wait a bit and try again. (Note, though, that the queue for this channel, CHAN_QUEUES[name], will keep filling up.)

⓭ As in our previous broker implementation, we do something special for channels whose name begins with /queue: we rotate the deque and send only to the first entry. This acts like a crude load-balancing system because each subscriber gets different messages off the same queue. For all other channels, all subscribers get all the messages.

⓮ We'll wait here for data on the queue, and exit if None is received. Currently, this isn't triggered anywhere (so these chan_sender() coroutines live forever), but if logic were added to clean up these channel tasks after, say, some period of inactivity, that's how it would be done.

⓯ Data has been received, so it's time to send to subscribers. We do not do the sending here: instead, we place the data onto each subscriber's own send queue. This decoupling is necessary to make sure that a slow subscriber doesn't slow down anyone else receiving data. And furthermore, if the subscriber is so slow that their send queue fills up, we don't put that data on their queue; i.e., it is lost.

The preceding design produces the same output as the earlier, simplistic implementation, but now we can be sure that a slow listener will not interfere with message distribution to other listeners.

These two case studies show a progression in thinking around the design of a message distribution system. A key aspect was the realization that sending and receiving data might be best handled in separate coroutines, depending on the use case. In such instances, queues can be very useful for moving data between those different coroutines and for providing buffering to decouple them.

The more important goal of these case studies was to show how the streams API in `asyncio` makes it very easy to build socket-based applications.

Twisted

The Twisted (*https://oreil.ly/Y3dY2*) project predates—dramatically—the `asyncio` standard library, and has been flying the flag of async programming in Python for around 14 years now. The project provides not only the basic building blocks, like an event loop, but also primitives like *deferreds* that are a bit like the futures in `asyncio`. The design of `asyncio` has been heavily influenced by Twisted and the extensive experience of its leaders and maintainers.

Note that `asyncio` does *not* replace Twisted (*https://oreil.ly/J0ezC*). Twisted includes high-quality implementations of a huge number of internet protocols, including not only the usual HTTP but also XMPP, NNTP, IMAP, SSH, IRC, and FTP (both servers and clients). And the list goes on: DNS? Check. SMTP? Check. POP3? Check. The availability of these excellent internet protocol implementations continues to make Twisted compelling.

At the code level, the main difference between Twisted and `asyncio`, apart from history and historical context, is that for a long time Python lacked language support for coroutines, and this meant that Twisted and projects like it had to figure out ways of dealing with asynchronicity that worked with standard Python syntax.

For most of Twisted's history, *callbacks* were the means by which async programming was done, with all the nonlinear complexity that entails; however, when it became possible to use generators as makeshift coroutines, it suddenly became possible to lay out code in Twisted in a linear fashion using its `@defer.inlineCallbacks` decorator, as shown in Example 4-10.

Example 4-10. Even more Twisted with inlined callbacks

```
@defer.inlineCallbacks   ❶
def f():
    yield
    defer.returnValue(123)   ❷

@defer.inlineCallbacks
def my_coro_func():
```

```
    value = yield f()  ❸
    assert value == 123
```

❶ Ordinarily, Twisted requires creating instances of Deferred and adding callbacks to those instances as the method of constructing async programs. A few years ago, the @inlineCallbacks decorator was added, which repurposes generators as coroutines.

❷ While @inlineCallbacks *did* allow you to write code that was linear in appearance (unlike callbacks), some hacks were required, such as this call to defer.returnValue(), which is how you have to return values from @inlineCallbacks coroutines.

❸ Here we can see the yield that makes this function a generator. For @inlineCallbacks to work, there must be at least one yield present in the function being decorated.

Since native coroutines appeared in Python 3.5, the Twisted team (and Amber Brown (*https://atleastfornow.net*) in particular) have been working to add support for running Twisted on the asyncio event loop.

This is an ongoing effort, and my goal in this section is not to convince you to create all your applications as Twisted-asyncio hybrids, but rather to make you aware that work is currently being done to provide significant interoperability between the two.

For those of you with experience using Twisted, Example 4-11 might be jarring.

Example 4-11. Support for asyncio in Twisted

```
# twisted_asyncio.py
from time import ctime
from twisted.internet import asyncioreactor
asyncioreactor.install()  ❶
from twisted.internet import reactor, defer, task  ❷

async def main():  ❸
    for i in range(5):
        print(f'{ctime()} Hello {i}')
        await task.deferLater(reactor, 1, lambda: None)  ❹

defer.ensureDeferred(main())  ❺
reactor.run()  ❻
```

❶ This is how you tell Twisted to use the asyncio event loop as its main reactor. Note that this line *must* come before the reactor is imported from twisted.internet on the following line.

---

❷ Anyone familiar with Twisted programming will recognize these imports. We don't have space to cover them in depth here, but in a nutshell, the reactor is the Twisted version of the asyncio *loop*, and defer and task are namespaces for tools to work with scheduling coroutines.

❸ Seeing async def here, in a Twisted program, looks odd, but this is indeed what the new support for async/await gives us: the ability to use native coroutines directly in Twisted programs.

❹ In the older @inlineCallbacks world, you would have used yield from here, but now we can use await, the same as in asyncio code. The other part of this line, deferLater(), is an alternative way to do the same thing as asyncio.sleep(1). We await a future where, after one second, a do-nothing callback will fire.

❺ ensureDeferred() is a Twisted version of scheduling a coroutine. This would be analogous to loop.create_task() or asyncio.ensure_future().

❻ Running the reactor is the same as loop.run_forever() in asyncio.

Running this script produces the following output:

```
$ twisted_asyncio.py
Mon Oct 16 16:19:49 2019 Hello 0
Mon Oct 16 16:19:50 2019 Hello 1
Mon Oct 16 16:19:51 2019 Hello 2
Mon Oct 16 16:19:52 2019 Hello 3
Mon Oct 16 16:19:53 2019 Hello 4
```

There's much more to learn about Twisted. In particular, it's well worth your time to go through the list of networking protocols it implements. There is still some work to be done, but the future looks very bright for interoperation between Twisted and asyncio.

asyncio has been designed in such a way that we can look forward to a future where it will be possible to incorporate code from many async frameworks, such as Twisted and Tornado, into a single application, with all code running on the same event loop.

The Janus Queue

The Janus queue (installed with `pip install janus`) provides a solution for communication between threads and coroutines. In the Python standard library, there are two kinds of queues:

`queue.Queue`
> A *blocking* queue, commonly used for communication and buffering between threads

`asyncio.Queue`
> An `async`-compatible queue, commonly used for communication and buffering between coroutines

Unfortunately, neither is useful for communication between threads and coroutines! This is where Janus comes in: it is a single queue that exposes both APIs, a blocking one *and* an async one. Example 4-12 generates data from inside a thread, places that data on a queue, and then consumes that data from a coroutine.

Example 4-12. Connecting coroutines and threads with a Janus queue

```
# janus_demo.py
import asyncio
import random
import time

import janus

async def main():
    loop = asyncio.get_running_loop()
    queue = janus.Queue(loop=loop)  ❶
    future = loop.run_in_executor(None, data_source, queue)
    while (data := await queue.async_q.get()) is not None:  ❷
        print(f'Got {data} off queue')  ❸
    print('Done.')

def data_source(queue):
    for i in range(10):
        r = random.randint(0, 4)
        time.sleep(r)  ❹
        queue.sync_q.put(r)  ❺
    queue.sync_q.put(None)

asyncio.run(main())
```

❶ Create a Janus queue. Note that just like an `asyncio.Queue`, the Janus queue will be associated with a specific event loop. As usual, if you don't provide the `loop` parameter, the standard `get_event_loop()` call will be used internally.

❷ Our main() coroutine function simply waits for data on a queue. This line will suspend until there is data, exactly until there is data, exactly like calling get() on an asyncio.Queue instance. The queue object has two *faces*: this one is called async_q and provides the async-compatible queue API.

❸ Print a message.

❹ Inside the data_source() function, a random int is generated, which is used both as a sleep duration and a data value. Note that the time.sleep() call is blocking, so this function must be executed in a thread.

❺ Place the data onto the Janus queue. This shows the other *face* of the Janus queue: sync_q, which provides the standard, blocking Queue API.

Here's the output:

```
$ <name>
Got 2 off queue
Got 4 off queue
Got 4 off queue
Got 2 off queue
Got 3 off queue
Got 4 off queue
Got 1 off queue
Got 1 off queue
Got 0 off queue
Got 4 off queue
Done.
```

If you can, it's better to aim for having short executor jobs, and in these cases, a queue (for communication) won't be necessary. This isn't always possible, though, and in such situations, the Janus queue can be the most convenient solution to buffer and distribute data between threads and coroutines.

aiohttp

aiohttp brings all things HTTP to asyncio, including support for HTTP clients and servers, as well as WebSocket support. Let's jump straight into code examples, starting with simplicity itself: "Hello World."

Case Study: Hello World

Example 4-13 shows a minimal web server using `aiohttp`.

Example 4-13. Minimal aiohttp example

```
from aiohttp import web

async def hello(request):
    return web.Response(text="Hello, world")

app = web.Application()  ❶
app.router.add_get('/', hello)  ❷
web.run_app(app, port=8080)  ❸
```

❶ An `Application` instance is created.

❷ A route is created, with the target coroutine `hello()` given as the handler.

❸ The web application is run.

Observe that there is no mention of loops, tasks, or futures in this code: the developers of the `aiohttp` framework have hidden all that away from us, leaving a very clean API. This is going to be common in most frameworks that build on top of `asyncio`, which has been designed to allow framework designers to choose only the bits they need, and encapsulate them in their preferred API.

Case Study: Scraping the News

`aiohttp` can be used both as a server and a client library, like the very popular (but blocking!) `requests` (*https://oreil.ly/E2s9d*) library. I wanted to showcase `aiohttp` by using an example that incorporates both features.

In this case study, we'll implement a website that does web scraping behind the scenes. The application will scrape two news websites and combine the headlines into one page of results. Here is the strategy:

1. A browser client makes a web request to *http://localhost:8080/news*.
2. Our web server receives the request, and then on the backend fetches HTML data from multiple news websites.
3. Each page's data is scraped for headlines.
4. The headlines are sorted and formatted into the response HTML that we send back to the browser client.

Figure 4-1 shows the output.

Figure 4-1. The final product of our news scraper: headlines from CNN are shown in one color, and Al Jazeera in another

Web scraping has become quite difficult nowadays. For example, if you try `requests.get('http://edition.cnn.com')`, you're going to find that the response contains very little usable data! It has become increasingly necessary to be able to execute JavaScript locally in order to obtain data, because many sites use JavaScript to load their actual content. The process of executing such JavaScript to produce the final, complete HTML output is called *rendering*.

To accomplish rendering, we use a neat project called Splash (*https://oreil.ly/1IAie*), which describes itself as a "JavaScript rendering service." It can run in a Docker (*https://www.docker.com*) container and provides an API for rendering other sites. Internally, it uses a (JavaScript-capable) WebKit engine to fully load and render a website. This is what we'll use to obtain website data. Our `aiohttp` server, shown in Example 4-14, will call this Splash API to obtain the page data.

To obtain and run the Splash container, run these commands in your shell:

```
$ docker pull scrapinghub/splash
$ docker run --rm -p 8050:8050 scrapinghub/splash
```

Our server backend will call the Splash API at *http://localhost:8050*.

Example 4-14. Code for the news scraper

```python
from asyncio import gather, create_task
from string import Template
from aiohttp import web, ClientSession
from bs4 import BeautifulSoup

async def news(request):  ❶
    sites = [
        ('http://edition.cnn.com', cnn_articles),  ❷
        ('http://www.aljazeera.com', aljazeera_articles),
    ]
    tasks = [create_task(news_fetch(*s)) for s in sites]  ❸
    await gather(*tasks)  ❹

    items = {  ❺
        text: (  ❻
            f'<div class="box {kind}">'
            f'<span>'
            f'<a href="{href}">{text}</a>'
            f'</span>'
            f'</div>'
        )
        for task in tasks for href, text, kind in task.result()
    }
    content = ''.join(items[x] for x in sorted(items))

    page = Template(open('index.html').read())  ❼
    return web.Response(
        body=page.safe_substitute(body=content),  ❽
        content_type='text/html',
    )

async def news_fetch(url, postprocess):
    proxy_url = (
        f'http://localhost:8050/render.html?'  ❾
        f'url={url}&timeout=60&wait=1'
    )
    async with ClientSession() as session:
        async with session.get(proxy_url) as resp:  ❿
            data = await resp.read()
            data = data.decode('utf-8')
    return postprocess(url, data)  ⓫
```

```
def cnn_articles(url, page_data):  ⑫
    soup = BeautifulSoup(page_data, 'lxml')
    def match(tag):
        return (
            tag.text and tag.has_attr('href')
            and tag['href'].startswith('/')
            and tag['href'].endswith('.html')
            and tag.find(class_='cd__headline-text')
        )
    headlines = soup.find_all(match)  ⑬
    return [(url + hl['href'], hl.text, 'cnn')
            for hl in headlines]

def aljazeera_articles(url, page_data):  ⑭
    soup = BeautifulSoup(page_data, 'lxml')
    def match(tag):
        return (
            tag.text and tag.has_attr('href')
            and tag['href'].startswith('/news')
            and tag['href'].endswith('.html')
        )
    headlines = soup.find_all(match)
    return [(url + hl['href'], hl. text, 'aljazeera')
            for hl in headlines]

app = web.Application()
app.router.add_get('/news', news)
web.run_app(app, port=8080)
```

❶ The news() function is the handler for the */news* URL on our server. It returns the HTML page showing all the headlines.

❷ Here, we have only two news websites to be scraped: CNN and Al Jazeera. More could easily be added, but then additional postprocessors would also have to be added, just like the cnn_articles() and aljazeera_articles() functions that are customized to extract headline data.

❸ For each news site, we create a task to fetch and process the HTML page data for its front page. Note that we unpack the tuple ((*s)) since the news_fetch() coroutine function takes both the URL and the postprocessing function as parameters. Each news_fetch() call will return a *list of tuples* as headline results, in the form *<article URL>, <article title>*.

❹ All the tasks are gathered together into a single Future (gather() returns a future representing the state of all the tasks being gathered), and then we immediately await the completion of that future. This line will suspend until the future completes.

❺ Since all the `news_fetch()` tasks are now complete, we collect all of the results into a dictionary. Note how nested comprehensions are used to iterate over tasks, and then over the list of tuples returned by each task. We also use *f-strings* to substitute data directly, including even the kind of page, which will be used in CSS to color the `div` background.

❻ In this dictionary, the *key* is the headline title, and the *value* is an HTML string for a `div` that will be displayed in our result page.

❼ Our web server is going to return HTML. We're loading HTML data from a local file called *index.html*. This file is presented in Example B-1 if you want to re-create the case study yourself.

❽ We substitute the collected headline `div` into the template and return the page to the browser client. This generates the page shown in Figure 4-1.

❾ Here, inside the `news_fetch()` coroutine function, we have a tiny template for hitting the Splash API (which, for me, is running in a local Docker container on port 8050). This demonstrates how `aiohttp` can be used as an HTTP client.

❿ The standard way is to create a `ClientSession()` instance, and then use the `get()` method on the session instance to perform the REST call. In the next line, the response data is obtained. Note that because we're always operating on coroutines, with `async with` and `await`, this coroutine will never block: we'll be able to handle many thousands of these requests, even though this operation (`news_fetch()`) might be relatively slow since we're doing web calls internally.

⓫ After the data is obtained, we call the postprocessing function. For CNN, it'll be `cnn_articles()`, and for Al Jazeera it'll be `aljazeera_articles()`.

⓬ We have space only for a brief look at the postprocessing. After getting the page data, we use the Beautiful Soup 4 library for extracting headlines.

⓭ The `match()` function will return all matching tags (I've manually checked the HTML source of these news websites to figure out which combination of filters extracts the best tags), and then we return a list of tuples matching the format *<article URL>, <article title>*.

⓮ This is the analogous postprocessor for Al Jazeera. The `match()` condition is slightly different, but it is otherwise the same as the CNN one.

Generally, you'll find that `aiohttp` has a simple API and "stays out of your way" while you develop your applications.

In the next section, we'll look at using ZeroMQ with `asyncio`, which has the curious effect of making socket programming quite enjoyable.

ØMQ (ZeroMQ)

> Programming is a science dressed up as art, because most of us don't understand the physics of software and it's rarely, if ever, taught. The physics of software is not algorithms, data structures, languages, and abstractions. These are just tools we make, use, and throw away. The real physics of software is the physics of people. Specifically, it's about our limitations when it comes to complexity and our desire to work together to solve large problems in pieces. This is the science of programming: make building blocks that people can understand and use easily, and people will work together to solve the very largest problems.
>
> —Pieter Hintjens, *ZeroMQ: Messaging for Many Applications*

ØMQ (or ZeroMQ (*http://zeromq.org*)) is a popular language-agnostic library for networking applications: it provides "smart" sockets. When you create ØMQ sockets in code, they resemble regular sockets, with recognizable method names like `recv()` and `send()` and so on—but internally these sockets handle some of the more annoying and tedious tasks required for working with conventional sockets.

One of the features it provides is management of message passing, so you don't have to invent your own protocol and count bytes on the wire to figure out when all the bytes for a particular message have arrived—you simply send whatever you consider to be a "message," and the whole thing arrives on the other end intact.

Another great feature is automatic reconnection logic. If the server goes down and comes back up later, the client ØMQ socket will *automatically* reconnect. And even better, messages your code sends into the socket will be buffered during the disconnected period, so they will all still be sent out when the server returns. These are some of the reasons ØMQ is sometimes referred to as *brokerless* messaging (*https://oreil.ly/oQE4x*): it provides some of the features of message broker software directly in the socket objects themselves.

ØMQ sockets are already implemented as asynchronous internally (so they can maintain many thousands of concurrent connections, even when used in threaded code), but this is hidden from us behind the ØMQ API. Nevertheless, support for Asyncio has been added to the PyZMQ (*https://oreil.ly/N8w7J*) Python bindings for the ØMQ library, and in this section we're going to look at several examples of how you might incorporate these smart sockets into your Python applications.

Case Study: Multiple Sockets

Here's a head-scratcher: if ØMQ provides sockets that are already asynchronous, in a way that is usable with threading, what is the point of using ØMQ with asyncio? The answer is cleaner code.

To demonstrate, let's look at a tiny case study in which you use multiple ØMQ sockets in the same application. First, Example 4-15 shows the blocking version (this example is taken from the zguide (*https://oreil.ly/qXAj8*), the official guide for ØMQ).

Example 4-15. The traditional ØMQ approach

```python
# poller.py
import zmq

context = zmq.Context()
receiver = context.socket(zmq.PULL)      ❶
receiver.connect("tcp://localhost:5557")

subscriber = context.socket(zmq.SUB)     ❷
subscriber.connect("tcp://localhost:5556")
subscriber.setsockopt_string(zmq.SUBSCRIBE, '')

poller = zmq.Poller()                    ❸
poller.register(receiver, zmq.POLLIN)
poller.register(subscriber, zmq.POLLIN)

while True:
    try:
        socks = dict(poller.poll())      ❹
    except KeyboardInterrupt:
        break

    if receiver in socks:
        message = receiver.recv_json()
        print(f'Via PULL: {message}')

    if subscriber in socks:
        message = subscriber.recv_json()
        print(f'Via SUB: {message}')
```

❶ ØMQ sockets have *types*. This is a PULL socket. You can think of it as a *receive-only* kind of socket that will be fed by some other *send-only* socket, which will be a PUSH type.

❷ The SUB socket is another kind of receive-only socket, and it will be fed a PUB socket which is send-only.

❸ If you need to move data between multiple sockets in a threaded ØMQ application, you're going to need a *poller*. This is because these sockets are not thread-safe, so you cannot `recv()` on different sockets in different threads.[1]

❹ It works similarly to the `select()` system call. The poller will unblock when there is data ready to be received on one of the registered sockets, and then it's up to you to pull the data off and do something with it. The big `if` block is how you detect the correct socket.

Using a poller loop plus an explicit socket-selection block makes the code look a little clunky, but this approach avoids thread-safety problems by guaranteeing the same socket is not used from different threads.

Example 4-16 shows the server code.

Example 4-16. Server code

```
# poller_srv.py
import zmq, itertools, time

context = zmq.Context()
pusher = context.socket(zmq.PUSH)
pusher.bind("tcp://*:5557")

publisher = context.socket(zmq.PUB)
publisher.bind("tcp://*:5556")

for i in itertools.count():
    time.sleep(1)
    pusher.send_json(i)
    publisher.send_json(i)
```

This code is not important for the discussion, but briefly: there's a PUSH socket and a PUB socket, as I said earlier, and a loop inside that sends data to both sockets every second. Here's sample output from *poller.py* (note: *both* programs must be running):

```
$ poller.py
Via PULL: 0
Via SUB: 0
Via PULL: 1
Via SUB: 1
Via PULL: 2
Via SUB: 2
```

---

1 Actually, you *can* as long as the sockets being used in different threads are created, used, and destroyed entirely in their own threads. It is possible but hard to do, and many people struggle to get this right. This is why the recommendation to use a single thread and a polling mechanism is so strong.

```
Via PULL: 3
Via SUB: 3
```

The code works; however, our interest here is not whether the code runs, but rather whether `asyncio` has anything to offer for the structure of *poller.py*. The key thing to understand is that our `asyncio` code is going to run in a single thread, which means that it's fine to handle different sockets in different *coroutines*—and indeed, this is exactly what we'll do.

Of course, someone had to do the hard work (*http://bit.ly/2sPCihI*) to add support for coroutines into pyzmq (the Python client library for ØMQ) itself for this to work, so it wasn't free. But we can take advantage of that hard work to improve on the "traditional" code structure, as shown in Example 4-17.

Example 4-17. Clean separation with asyncio

```python
# poller_aio.py
import asyncio
import zmq
from zmq.asyncio import Context

context = Context()

async def do_receiver():
    receiver = context.socket(zmq.PULL)     ❶
    receiver.connect("tcp://localhost:5557")
    while message := await receiver.recv_json():    ❷
        print(f'Via PULL: {message}')

async def do_subscriber():
    subscriber = context.socket(zmq.SUB)     ❸
    subscriber.connect("tcp://localhost:5556")
    subscriber.setsockopt_string(zmq.SUBSCRIBE, '')
    while message := await subscriber.recv_json():   ❹
        print(f'Via SUB: {message}')

async def main():
    await asyncio.gather(
        do_receiver(),
        do_subscriber(),
    )

asyncio.run(main())
```

❶ This code sample does the same as Example 4-15, except that now we're taking advantage of coroutines to restructure everything. Now we can deal with each socket in isolation. I've created two coroutine functions, one for each socket; this one is for the PULL socket.

❷ I'm using the asyncio support in pyzmq, which means that all send() and recv() calls must use the await keyword. The Poller no longer appears anywhere, because it's been integrated into the asyncio event loop itself.

❸ This is the handler for the SUB socket. The structure is very similar to the PULL socket's handler, but that need not have been the case. If more complex logic had been required, I'd have been able to easily add it here, fully encapsulated within the SUB-handler code only.

❹ Again, the asyncio-compatible sockets require the await keyword to send and receive.

The output is the same as before, so I won't show it.

The use of coroutines has, in my opinion, a staggeringly positive effect on the code layout in these examples. In real production code with lots of ØMQ sockets, the coroutine handlers for each could even be in separate files, providing more opportunities for better code structure. And even for programs with a single read/write socket, it is very easy to use separate coroutines for reading and writing, if necessary.

The improved code looks a lot like threaded code, and indeed, for the specific example shown here, the same refactor will work for threading: run blocking do_receiver() and do_subscriber() functions in separate threads. But do you really want to deal with even the *potential* for race conditions, especially as your application grows in features and complexity over time?

There is lots to explore here, and as I said before, these magic sockets are a lot of fun to play with. In the next case study, we'll look at a more practical use of ØMQ.

Case Study: Application Performance Monitoring

With the modern, containerized, microservice-based deployment practices of today, some things that used to be trivial, such as monitoring your apps' CPU and memory usage, have become somewhat more complicated than just running top. Several commercial products have emerged over the last few years to deal with these problems, but their cost can be prohibitive for small startup teams and hobbyists.

In this case study, I'll exploit ØMQ and asyncio to build a toy prototype for distributed application monitoring. Our design has three parts:

Application layer
    This layer contains all our applications. Examples might be a "customers" microservice, a "bookings" microservice, an "emailer" microservice, and so on. I will add a ØMQ "transmitting" socket to each of our applications. This socket will send performance metrics to a central server.

Collection layer

The central server will expose a ØMQ socket to collect the data from all the running application instances. The server will also serve a web page to show performance graphs over time and will live-stream the data as it comes in.

Visualization layer

This is the web page being served. We'll display the collected data in a set of charts, and the charts will live-update in real time. To simplify the code samples, I will use the convenient Smoothie Charts (*http://smoothiecharts.org*) JavaScript library, which provides all the necessary client-side features.

The backend app (application layer) that produces metrics is shown in Example 4-18.

Example 4-18. The application layer: producing metrics

```python
import argparse
import asyncio
from random import randint, uniform
from datetime import datetime as dt
from datetime import timezone as tz
from contextlib import suppress
import zmq, zmq.asyncio, psutil

ctx = zmq.asyncio.Context()

async def stats_reporter(color: str):     ❶
    p = psutil.Process()
    sock = ctx.socket(zmq.PUB)     ❷
    sock.setsockopt(zmq.LINGER, 1)
    sock.connect('tcp://localhost:5555')     ❸
    with suppress(asyncio.CancelledError):     ❹
        while True:     ❺
            await sock.send_json(dict(     ❻
                color=color,
                timestamp=dt.now(tz=tz.utc).isoformat(),     ❼
                cpu=p.cpu_percent(),
                mem=p.memory_full_info().rss / 1024 / 1024
            ))
            await asyncio.sleep(1)
    sock.close()     ❽

async def main(args):
    asyncio.create_task(stats_reporter(args.color))
    leak = []
    with suppress(asyncio.CancelledError):
        while True:
            sum(range(randint(1_000, 10_000_000)))     ❾
            await asyncio.sleep(uniform(0, 1))
            leak += [0] * args.leak
```

```
if __name__ == '__main__':
    parser = argparse.ArgumentParser()
    parser.add_argument('--color', type=str)  ❿
    parser.add_argument('--leak', type=int, default=0)
    args = parser.parse_args()
    try:
        asyncio.run(main(args))
    except KeyboardInterrupt:
        print('Leaving...')
        ctx.term()  ⓫
```

❶ This coroutine function will run as a long-lived coroutine, continually sending out data to the server process.

❷ Create a ØMQ socket. As you know, there are different flavors of socket; this one is a PUB type, which allows one-way messages to be sent to another ØMQ socket. This socket has—as the ØMQ guide says—superpowers. It will automatically handle all reconnection and buffering logic for us.

❸ Connect to the server.

❹ Our shutdown sequence is driven by KeyboardInterrupt, farther down. When that signal is received, all the tasks will be cancelled. Here I handle the raised CancelledError with the handy suppress() context manager from the context lib standard library module.

❺ Iterate forever, sending out data to the server.

❻ Since ØMQ knows how to work with complete messages, and not just chunks off a bytestream, it opens the door to a bunch of useful wrappers around the usual sock.send() idiom: here, I use one of those helper methods, send_json(), which will automatically serialize the argument into JSON. This allows us to use a dict() directly.

❼ A reliable way to transmit datetime information is via the ISO 8601 format. This is especially true if you have to pass datetime data between software written in different languages, since the vast majority of language implementations will be able to work with this standard.

❽ To end up here, we must have received the CancelledError exception resulting from task cancellation. The ØMQ socket must be closed to allow program shutdown.

❾ The main() function symbolizes the actual microservice application. Fake work is produced with this sum over random numbers, just to give us some nonzero data to view in the visualization layer a bit later.

❿ I'm going to create multiple instances of this application, so it will be convenient to be able to distinguish between them (later, in the graphs) with a --color parameter.

⓫ Finally, the ØMQ context can be terminated.

The primary point of interest is the stats_reporter() function. This is what streams out metrics data (collected by the useful psutil library). The rest of the code can be assumed to be a typical microservice application.

The server code in Example 4-19 collects all the data and serves it to a web client.

Example 4-19. The collection layer: this server collects process stats

```python
# metric-server.py
import asyncio
from contextlib import suppress
import zmq
import zmq.asyncio
import aiohttp
from aiohttp import web
from aiohttp_sse import sse_response
from weakref import WeakSet
import json

# zmq.asyncio.install()
ctx = zmq.asyncio.Context()
connections = WeakSet()  ❶

async def collector():
    sock = ctx.socket(zmq.SUB)  ❷
    sock.setsockopt_string(zmq.SUBSCRIBE, '')  ❸
    sock.bind('tcp://*:5555')  ❹
    with suppress(asyncio.CancelledError):
        while data := await sock.recv_json():  ❺
            print(data)
            for q in connections:
                await q.put(data)  ❻
    sock.close()

async def feed(request):  ❼
    queue = asyncio.Queue()
    connections.add(queue)  ❽
    with suppress(asyncio.CancelledError):
        async with sse_response(request) as resp:  ❾
```

```
            while data := await queue.get():  ❿
                print('sending data:', data)
                resp.send(json.dumps(data))  ⓫
    return resp

async def index(request):  ⓬
    return aiohttp.web.FileResponse('./charts.html')

async def start_collector(app):  ⓭
    app['collector'] = app.loop.create_task(collector())

async def stop_collector(app):
    print('Stopping collector...')
    app['collector'].cancel()  ⓮
    await app['collector']
    ctx.term()

if __name__ == '__main__':
    app = web.Application()
    app.router.add_route('GET', '/', index)
    app.router.add_route('GET', '/feed', feed)
    app.on_startup.append(start_collector)  ⓯
    app.on_cleanup.append(stop_collector)
    web.run_app(app, host='127.0.0.1', port=8088)
```

❶ One half of this program will receive data from other applications, and the other half will provide data to browser clients via *server-sent events* (SSEs). I use a WeakSet() to keep track of all the currently connected web clients. Each connected client will have an associated Queue() instance, so this connections identifier is really a set of queues.

❷ Recall that in the application layer, I used a zmq.PUB socket; here in the collection layer, I use its partner, the zmq.SUB socket type. This ØMQ socket can only receive, not send.

❸ For the zmq.SUB socket type, providing a subscription name is required, but for our purposes, we'll just take everything that comes in—hence the empty topic name.

❹ I *bind* the zmq.SUB socket. Think about that for second. In pub-sub configurations, you usually have to make the *pub* end the server (bind()) and the *sub* end the client (connect()). ØMQ is different: either end can be the server. For our use case, this is important, because each of our application-layer instances will be connecting to the same collection server domain name, and not the other way around.

❺ The support for `asyncio` in `pyzmq` allows us to `await` data from our connected apps. And not only that, but the incoming data will be automatically deserialized from JSON (yes, this means `data` is a `dict()`).

❻ Recall that our `connections` set holds a queue for every connected web client. Now that data has been received, it's time to send it to all the clients: the data is placed onto each queue.

❼ The `feed()` coroutine function will create coroutines for each connected web client. Internally, server-sent events (*https://mzl.la/2omEs3t*) are used to push data to the web clients.

❽ As described earlier, each web client will have its own `queue` instance, in order to receive data from the `collector()` coroutine. The `queue` instance is added to the `connections` set, but because `connections` is a *weak* set, the entry will automatically be removed from `connections` when the `queue` goes out of scope—i.e., when a web client disconnects. Weakrefs (*https://oreil.ly/fRmdu*) are great for simplifying these kinds of bookkeeping tasks.

❾ The `aiohttp_sse` package provides the `sse_response()` context manager. This gives us a scope inside which to push data to the web client.

❿ We remain connected to the web client, and wait for data on this specific client's queue.

⓫ As soon as the data comes in (inside `collector()`), it will be sent to the connected web client. Note that I reserialize the `data` dict here. An optimization to this code would be to avoid deserializing JSON in `collector()`, and instead use `sock.recv_string()` to avoid the serialization round trip. Of course, in a real scenario, you might want to deserialize in the collector, and perform some validation on the data before sending it to the browser client. So many choices!

⓬ The `index()` endpoint is the primary page load, and here we serve a static file called *charts.html*.

⓭ The `aiohttp` library provides facilities for us to hook in additional long-lived coroutines we might need. With the `collector()` coroutine, we have exactly that situation, so I create a startup coroutine, `start_collector()`, and a shutdown coroutine. These will be called during specific phases of `aiohttp`'s startup and shutdown sequence. Note that I add the collector task to the `app` itself, which implements a mapping protocol so that you can use it like a dict.

⓮ I obtain our `collector()` coroutine off the `app` identifier and call `cancel()` on that.

⓯ Finally, you can see where the custom startup and shutdown coroutines are hooked in: the `app` instance provides hooks to which our custom coroutines may be appended.

All that remains is the visualization layer, shown in Example 4-20. I'm using the Smoothie Charts library (*http://smoothiecharts.org*) to generate scrolling charts, and the complete HTML for our main (and only) web page, *charts.html*, is provided in the Example B-1. There is too much HTML, CSS, and JavaScript to present in this section, but I do want to highlight a few points about how the server-sent events are handled in JavaScript in the browser client.

Example 4-20. The visualization layer, which is a fancy way of saying "the browser"

```
<snip>
var evtSource = new EventSource("/feed");  ❶
evtSource.onmessage = function(e) {
    var obj = JSON.parse(e.data);  ❷
    if (!(obj.color in cpu)) {
        add_timeseries(cpu, cpu_chart, obj.color);
    }
    if (!(obj.color in mem)) {
        add_timeseries(mem, mem_chart, obj.color);
    }
    cpu[obj.color].append(
        Date.parse(obj.timestamp), obj.cpu);  ❸
    mem[obj.color].append(
        Date.parse(obj.timestamp), obj.mem);
};
<snip>
```

❶ Create a new `EventSource()` instance on the */feed* URL. The browser will connect to */feed* on our server, (*metric_server.py*). Note that the browser will automatically try to reconnect if the connection is lost. Server-sent events are often overlooked, but in many situations their simplicity makes them preferable to WebSockets.

❷ The `onmessage` event will fire every time the server sends data. Here the data is parsed as JSON.

❸ The `cpu` identifier is a mapping of a color to a `TimeSeries()` instance (for more on this, see Example B-1). Here, we obtain that time series and append data to it.

We also obtain the timestamp and parse it to get the correct format required by the chart.

Now we can run the code. To get the whole show moving, a bunch of command-line instructions are required, the first of which is to start up the data collector process:

```
$ metric-server.py
======== Running on http://127.0.0.1:8088 ========
(Press CTRL+C to quit)
```

The next step is to start up all the microservice instances. These will send their CPU and memory usage metrics to the collector. Each will be identified by a different color, which is specified on the command line. Note how two of the microservices are told to leak some memory:

```
$ backend-app.py --color red &
$ backend-app.py --color blue --leak 10000 &
$ backend-app.py --color green --leak 100000 &
```

Figure 4-2 shows our final product in a browser. You'll have to take my word for it that the graphs really do animate. You'll notice in the preceding command lines that I added some memory leakage to blue, and a lot to green. I even had to restart the green service a few times to prevent it from climbing over 100 MB.

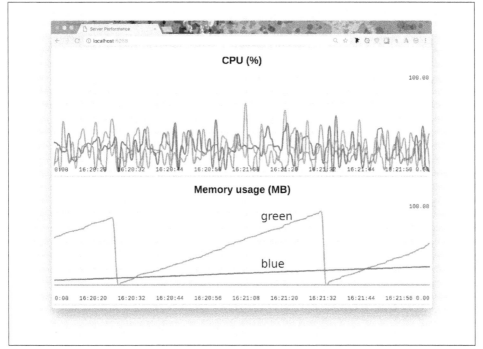

Figure 4-2. We'd better get an SRE on green ASAP!

What is especially interesting about this project is this: *any* of the running instances in any part of this stack can be restarted, and no reconnect-handling code is necessary. The ØMQ sockets, along with the `EventSource()` JavaScript instance in the browser, magically reconnect and pick up where they left off.

In the next section, we turn our attention to databases and to how `asyncio` might be used to design a system for cache invalidation.

asyncpg and Sanic

The `asyncpg` library (*https://oreil.ly/yGdNh*) provides client access to the PostgreSQL database, but differentiates itself from other `asyncio`-compatible Postgres client libraries with its emphasis on speed. `asyncpg` is authored by Yury Selivanov (*https://twitter.com/1st1*), one of the core `asyncio` Python developers, who is also the author of the uvloop project. It has no third-party dependencies, although Cython (*http://cython.org*) is required if you're installing from source.

`asyncpg` achieves its speed by working directly against the PostgreSQL binary protocol, and other advantages to this low-level approach include support for prepared statements (*http://bit.ly/2sMNlIz*) and scrollable cursors (*http://bit.ly/2Chr0H5*).

We'll be looking at a case study using `asyncpg` for cache invalidation, but before that it will be useful to get a basic understanding of the API `asyncpg` provides. For all of the code in this section, we'll need a running instance of PostgreSQL. This is most easily done with Docker, using the following command:

```
$ docker run -d --rm -p 55432:5432 postgres
```

Note that I've exposed port 55432 rather than the default, 5432, just in case you already have a running instance of the database on the default port. Example 4-21 briefly demonstrates how to use `asyncpg` to talk to PostgreSQL.

Example 4-21. Basic demo of asyncpg

```
# asyncpg-basic.py
import asyncio
import asyncpg
import datetime
from util import Database        ❶

async def main():
    async with Database('test', owner=True) as conn:    ❷
        await demo(conn)

async def demo(conn: asyncpg.Connection):
    await conn.execute('''
        CREATE TABLE users(
```

```
            id serial PRIMARY KEY,
            name text,
            dob date
        )'''
    )  ❸

    pk = await conn.fetchval(  ❹
        'INSERT INTO users(name, dob) VALUES($1, $2) '
        'RETURNING id', 'Bob', datetime.date(1984, 3, 1)
    )

    async def get_row():  ❺
        return await conn.fetchrow(  ❻
            'SELECT * FROM users WHERE name = $1',
            'Bob'
        )
    print('After INSERT:', await get_row())  ❼

    await conn.execute(
        'UPDATE users SET dob = $1 WHERE id=1',
        datetime.date(1985, 3, 1)  ❽
    )
    print('After UPDATE:', await get_row())

    await conn.execute(
        'DELETE FROM users WHERE id=1'
    )
    print('After DELETE:', await get_row())

if __name__ == '__main__':
    asyncio.run(main())
```

❶   I've hidden some boilerplate away in a tiny util module to simplify things and keep the core message.

❷   The Database class gives us a context manager that will create a new database for us—in this, case named test—and will destroy that database when the context manager exits. This turns out to be very useful when experimenting with ideas in code. Because no state is carried over between experiments, you start from a clean database every time. Note that this is an async with context manager; we'll talk more about that later, but for now, the focal area of this demo is what happens inside the demo() coroutine.

❸   The Database context manager has provided us with a Connection instance, which is immediately used to create a new table, users.

❹ I use `fetchval()` to insert a new record. While I could have used `execute()` to do the insertion, the benefit of using `fetchval()` is that I can obtain the `id` of the newly inserted record, which I store in the `pk` identifier.

Note that I use *parameters* (`$1` and `$2`) for passing data to the SQL query. *Never* use string interpolation or concatenation to build queries, as this is a security risk!

❺ In the remainder of this demo, I'm going to be manipulating data in the `users` table, so here I make a new utility coroutine function that fetches a record in the table. This will be called several times.

❻ When *retrieving* data, it is far more useful to use the `fetch`-based methods, because these will return `Record` objects. `asyncpg` will automatically cast data-types to the most appropriate types for Python.

❼ I immediately use the `get_row()` helper to display the newly inserted record.

❽ I modify data by using the `UPDATE` command for SQL. It's a tiny modification: the year value in the date of birth is changed by one year. As before, this is performed with the connection's `execute()` method. The remainder of the code demo fol-lows the same structure as seen so far, and a `DELETE`, followed by another `print()`, happens a few lines down.

Here's the output of running this script:

```
$ asyncpg-basic.py
After INSERT: <Record id=1 name='Bob' dob=datetime.date(1984, 3, 1)>
After UPDATE: <Record id=1 name='Bob' dob=datetime.date(1985, 3, 1)>
After DELETE: None
```

Note how the date value retrieved in our `Record` object has been converted to a Python `date` object: `asyncpg` has automatically converted the datatype from the SQL type to its Python counterpart. A large table of type conversions (*http://bit.ly/ 2sQszaQ*) in the `asyncpg` documentation describes all the type mappings that are built into the library.

The preceding code is very simple, perhaps even crudely so if you're used to the con-venience of object-relational mappers (ORMs) like SQLAlchemy or the Django web framework's built-in ORM. At the end of this chapter, I mention several third-party libraries that provide access to ORMs or ORM-like features for `asyncpg`.

Example 4-22 shows my boilerplate `Database` object in the `utils` module; you may find it useful to make something similar for your own experiments.

Example 4-22. Useful tooling for your asyncpg experiments

```python
# util.py
import argparse, asyncio, asyncpg
from asyncpg.pool import Pool

DSN = 'postgresql://{user}@{host}:{port}'
DSN_DB = DSN + '/{name}'
CREATE_DB = 'CREATE DATABASE {name}'
DROP_DB = 'DROP DATABASE {name}'

class Database:
    def __init__(self, name, owner=False, **kwargs):
        self.params = dict(
            user='postgres', host='localhost',
            port=55432, name=name)             ❶
        self.params.update(kwargs)
        self.pool: Pool = None
        self.owner = owner
        self.listeners = []

    async def connect(self) -> Pool:
        if self.owner:
            await self.server_command(
                CREATE_DB.format(**self.params))   ❸

        self.pool = await asyncpg.create_pool(    ❹
            DSN_DB.format(**self.params))
        return self.pool

    async def disconnect(self):
        """Destroy the database"""
        if self.pool:
            releases = [self.pool.release(conn)
                        for conn in self.listeners]
            await asyncio.gather(*releases)
            await self.pool.close()           ❺
        if self.owner:
            await self.server_command(        ❻
                DROP_DB.format(**self.params))

    async def __aenter__(self) -> Pool:       ❷
        return await self.connect()

    async def __aexit__(self, *exc):
        await self.disconnect()

    async def server_command(self, cmd):      ❼
        conn = await asyncpg.connect(
            DSN.format(**self.params))
        await conn.execute(cmd)
        await conn.close()
```

```
    async def add_listener(self, channel, callback):  ❽
        conn: asyncpg.Connection = await self.pool.acquire()
        await conn.add_listener(channel, callback)
        self.listeners.append(conn)

if __name__ == '__main__':
    parser = argparse.ArgumentParser()
    parser.add_argument('--cmd', choices=['create', 'drop'])
    parser.add_argument('--name', type=str)
    args = parser.parse_args()
    d = Database(args.name, owner=True)
    if args.cmd == 'create':
        asyncio.run(d.connect())
    elif args.cmd == 'drop':
        asyncio.run(d.disconnect())
    else:
        parser.print_help()
```

❶ The Database class is just a fancy context manager for creating and deleting a
    database from a PostgreSQL instance. The database name is passed into the
    constructor.

❷ (Note: The sequence of callouts in the code is intentionally different from this
    list.) This is an *asynchronous* context manager. Instead of the usual __enter__()
    and __exit__() methods, I use their __aenter__() and __aexit__()
    counterparts.

❸ Here, in the entering side, I'll create the new database and return a connection to
    that new database. server_command() is another helper method defined a few
    lines down. I use it to run the command for creating our new database.

❹ I then make a connection to the newly created database. Note that I've hardcoded
    several details about the connection: this is intentional, as I wanted to keep the
    code samples small. You could easily generalize this by making fields for the user-
    name, hostname, and port.

❺ In the exiting side of the context manager, I close the connection and…

❻ …destroy the database.

❼ For completeness, this is our utility method for running commands against the
    PostgreSQL server itself. It creates a connection for that purpose, runs the given
    command, and exits.

➑ This function creates a long-lived socket connection to the database that will listen for events. This mechanism will be featured in the upcoming case study.

 In point 8 for the preceding code, I created a dedicated connection for each channel I want to listen on. This is expensive since it means that a PostgreSQL worker will be completely tied up for every channel being listened to. A much better design would be to use one connection for multiple channels. Once you have worked through this example, try to modify the code to use a single connection for multiple channel listeners.

Now that you have an understanding of the basic building blocks of `asyncpg`, we can explore it further with a really fun case study: using PostgreSQL's built-in support for sending event notifications to perform cache invalidation!

Case Study: Cache Invalidation

There are two hard things in computer science: cache invalidation, naming things, and off-by-one errors.

—Phil Karlton

It is common in web services and web applications that the persistence layer, i.e., the backing database (DB), becomes the performance bottleneck sooner than any other part of the stack. The application layer can usually be scaled horizontally by running more instances, whereas it's trickier to do that with a database.

This is why it's common practice to look at design options that can limit excessive interaction with the database. The most common option is to use *caching* to "remember" previously fetched database results and replay them when asked, thus avoiding subsequent calls to the DB for the same information.

However, what happens if one of your app instances writes new data to the database while another app instance is still returning the old, stale data from its internal cache? This is a classic *cache invalidation* problem, and it can be very difficult to resolve in a robust way.

Our attack strategy is as follows:

1. Each app instance has an in-memory cache of DB queries.

2. When one writes new data to the database, the database alerts all of the connected app instances of the new data.

3. Each app instance then updates its internal cache accordingly.

This case study will highlight how PostgreSQL, with its built-in support for event updates via the LISTEN (*http://bit.ly/2EP9yeJ*) and NOTIFY (*http://bit.ly/2BN5lp1*) commands, can simply *tell us* when its data has changed.

asyncpg already has support for the LISTEN/NOTIFY API. This feature of PostgreSQL allows your app to subscribe to events on a named channel and to post events to named channels. PostgreSQL can almost become a lighter version of RabbitMQ (*https://oreil.ly/jvDgm*) or ActiveMQ (*https://oreil.ly/yiaK0*)!

This case study has more moving parts than usual, and that makes it awkward to present in the usual linear format. Instead, we'll begin by looking at the final product, and work backward toward the underlying implementation.

Our app provides a JSON-based API server for managing the favorite dishes of patrons at our robotic restaurant. The backing database will have only one table, patron, with only two fields: name and fav_dish. Our API will allow the usual set of four operations: *create*, *read*, *update*, and *delete* (CRUD).

The following is a sample interaction with our API using curl, illustrating how to create a new entry in our database (I haven't yet shown how to start up the server running on *localhost:8000*; that will come later):

```
$ curl -d '{"name": "Carol", "fav_dish": "SPAM Bruschetta"}' \
    -H "Content-Type: application/json" \
    -X POST \
    http://localhost:8000/patron
{"msg":"ok","id":37}
```

The -d parameter is for data,[2] -H is for the HTTP headers, -X is for the HTTP request method (alternatives include GET, DELETE, PUT, and a few others), and the URL is for our API server. We'll get to the code for that shortly.

In the output, we see that the creation was ok, and the id being returned is the primary key of the new record in the database.

In the next few shell snippets, we'll run through the other three operations: *read*, *update*, and *delete*. We can read the patron record we just created with this command:

```
$ curl -X GET http://localhost:8000/patron/37

{"id":37,"name":"Carol","fav_dish":"SPAM Bruschetta"}
```

Reading the data is pretty straightforward. Note that the id of the desired record must be supplied in the URL.

---

2 The recipe for this dish, and recipes for other fine Spam-based fare, can be found on the UKTV website (*http://bit.ly/2CGymPL*).

Next, we'll update the record and check the results:

```
$ curl -d '{"name": "Eric", "fav_dish": "SPAM Bruschetta"}' \
    -H "Content-Type: application/json" \
    -X PUT \
    http://localhost:8000/patron/37
$ curl -X GET http://localhost:8000/patron/37
{"msg":"ok"}
{"id":37,"name":"Eric","fav_dish":"SPAM Bruschetta"}
```

Updating a resource is similar to creating one, with two key differences:

- The HTTP request method (-X) is PUT, not POST.
- The URL now requires the id field to specify which resource to update.

Finally, we can delete the record and verify its deletion with the following commands:

```
$ curl -X DELETE http://localhost:8000/patron/37
$ curl -X GET http://localhost:8000/patron/37
{"msg":"ok"}
null
```

As you can see, null is returned when you try to GET a record that doesn't exist.

So far this all looks quite ordinary, but our objective is not only to make a CRUD API —we want to look at cache invalidation. So, let's turn our attention toward the cache. Now that we have a basic understanding of our app's API, we can look at the application logs to see timing data for each request: this will tell us which requests are cached, and which hit the DB.

When the server is first started up, the cache is empty; it's a memory cache, after all. We're going to start up our server, and then in a separate shell run two GET requests in quick succession:

```
$ curl -X GET http://localhost:8000/patron/29
$ curl -X GET http://localhost:8000/patron/29
{"id":29,"name":"John Cleese","fav_dish":"Gravy on Toast"}
{"id":29,"name":"John Cleese","fav_dish":"Gravy on Toast"}
```

We expect that the first time we retrieve our record, there's going to be a cache miss, and the second time, a hit. We can see evidence of this in the log for the API server itself (the first Sanic web server, running on *localhost:8000*):

```
$ sanic_demo.py
2019-09-29 16:20:33 - (sanic)[DEBUG]:
```

```
2019-09-29 16:20:33 (sanic): Goin' Fast @ http://0.0.0.0:8000
2019-09-29 16:20:33 (sanic): Starting worker [10366]    ❶
2019-09-29 16:25:27 (perf): id=37 Cache miss    ❷
2019-09-29 16:25:27 (perf): get Elapsed: 4.26 ms    ❸
2019-09-29 16:25:27 (perf): get Elapsed: 0.04 ms    ❹
```

❶ Everything up to this line is the default `sanic` startup log message.

❷ As described, the first GET results in a cache miss because the server has only just started.

❸ This is from our first `curl -X GET`. I've added some timing functionality to the API endpoints. Here we can see that the handler for the GET request took ~4 ms.

❹ The second GET returns data from the cache, and the much faster (100x faster!) timing data.

So far, nothing unusual. Many web apps use caching in this way.

Now let's start up a second app instance on port 8001 (the first instance was on port 8000):

```
$ sanic_demo.py --port 8001
<snip>
```

```
2017-10-02 08:09:56 - (sanic): Goin' Fast @ http://0.0.0.0:8001
2017-10-02 08:09:56 - (sanic): Starting worker [385]
```

Both instances, of course, connect to the same database. Now, with both API server instances running, let's modify the data for patron *John*, who clearly lacks sufficient Spam in his diet. Here we perform an UPDATE against the first app instance at port 8000:

```
$ curl -d '{"name": "John Cleese", "fav_dish": "SPAM on toast"}' \
    -H "Content-Type: application/json" \
    -X PUT \
    http://localhost:8000/patron/29
{"msg":"ok"}
```

Immediately after this update event on only one of the app instances, *both* API servers, 8000 and 8001, report the event in their respective logs:

```
2019-10-02 08:35:49 - (perf)[INFO]: Got DB event:
{
    "table": "patron",
    "id": 29,
    "type": "UPDATE",
    "data": {
        "old": {
            "id": 29,
            "name": "John Cleese",
            "fav_dish": "Gravy on Toast"
        },
        "new": {
            "id": 29,
            "name": "John Cleese",
            "fav_dish": "SPAM on toast"
        },
        "diff": {
            "fav_dish": "SPAM on toast"
        }
    }
}
```

The database has reported the update event back to both app instances. We haven't done any requests against app instance 8001 yet, though—does this mean that the new data is already cached there?

To check, we can do a GET on the second server, at port 8001:

```
$ curl -X GET http://localhost:8001/patron/29
{"id":29,"name":"John Cleese","fav_dish":"SPAM on toast"}
```

The timing info in the log output shows that we do indeed obtain the data directly from the cache, even though this is our first request:

```
2019-10-02 08:46:45 - (perf)[INFO]: get Elapsed: 0.04 ms
```

The upshot is that when the database changes, *all connected app instances* get notified, allowing them to update their caches.

With this explanation out of the way, we can now look at the `asyncpg` code implementation required to make our cache invalidation actually work. The basic design for the server code shown in Example 4-23 is the following:

1. We have a simple web API using the new, `asyncio`-compatible Sanic web framework (*https://oreil.ly/q5eA4*).

2. The data will be stored in a backend PostgreSQL instance, but the API will be served via multiple instances of the web API app servers.

3. The app servers will cache data from the database.

4. The app servers will subscribe to events via `asyncpg` in specific tables on the DB, and will receive update notifications when the data in the DB table has been changed. This allows the app servers to update their individual in-memory caches.

Example 4-23. API server with Sanic

```
# sanic_demo.py
import argparse
from sanic import Sanic
from sanic.views import HTTPMethodView
from sanic.response import json
from util import Database        ❶
from perf import aelapsed, aprofiler    ❷
import model

app = Sanic()    ❸

@aelapsed
async def new_patron(request):    ❹
    data = request.json    ❺
    id = await model.add_patron(app.pool, data)    ❻
    return json(dict(msg='ok', id=id))    ❼

class PatronAPI(HTTPMethodView, metaclass=aprofiler):    ❽
    async def get(self, request, id):
        data = await model.get_patron(app.pool, id)    ❾
        return json(data)

    async def put(self, request, id):
        data = request.json
        ok = await model.update_patron(app.pool, id, data)
        return json(dict(msg='ok' if ok else 'bad'))    ❿
```

```
    async def delete(self, request, id):
        ok = await model.delete_patron(app.pool, id)
        return json(dict(msg='ok' if ok else 'bad'))

@app.listener('before_server_start')    ⓫
async def db_connect(app, loop):
    app.db = Database('restaurant', owner=False)    ⓬
    app.pool = await app.db.connect()    ⓭
    await model.create_table_if_missing(app.pool)    ⓮
    await app.db.add_listener('chan_patron', model.db_event)    ⓯

@app.listener('after_server_stop')    ⓰
async def db_disconnect(app, loop):
    await app.db.disconnect()

if __name__ == "__main__":
    parser = argparse.ArgumentParser()
    parser.add_argument('--port', type=int, default=8000)
    args = parser.parse_args()
    app.add_route(
        new_patron, '/patron', methods=['POST'])    ⓱
    app.add_route(
        PatronAPI.as_view(), '/patron/<id:int>')    ⓲
    app.run(host="0.0.0.0", port=args.port)
```

❶ The Database utility helper, as described earlier. This will provide the methods required to connect to the database.

❷ Two more tools I've cobbled together to log the elapsed time of each API endpoint. I used this in the previous discussion to detect when a GET was being returned from the cache. The implementations for aelapsed() and aprofiler() are not important for this case study, but you can obtain them in Example B-1.

❸ We create the main Sanic app instance.

❹ This coroutine function is for creating new patron entries. In an add_route() call toward the bottom of the code, new_patron() is associated with the endpoint /patron, only for the POST HTTP method. The @aelapsed decorator is not part of the Sanic API: it's my own invention, merely to log out timings for each call.

❺ Sanic provides immediate deserialization of received JSON data by using the .json attribute on the request object.

❻ The model module, which I imported, is the *model* for our patron table in the database. I'll go through that in more detail in the next code listing; for now, just understand that all the database queries and SQL are in this model module. Here

I'm passing the connection pool for the database, and the same pattern is used for all the interaction with the database model in this function and in the `PatronAPI` class further down.

❼ A new primary key, `id`, will be created, and this is returned back to the caller as JSON.

❽ While creation is handled in the `new_patron()` function, all other interactions are handled in this *class-based view*, which is a convenience provided by Sanic. All the methods in this class are associated with the same URL, `/patron/<id:int>`, which you can see in the `add_route()` function near the bottom. Note that the `id` URL parameter will be passed to each of the methods, and this parameter is required for all three endpoints.

You can safely ignore the `metaclass` argument: all it does is wrap each method with the `@aelapsed` decorator so that timings will be printed in the logs. Again, this is not part of the Sanic API; it's my own invention for logging timing data.

❾ As before, model interaction is performed inside the `model` module.

❿ If the model reports failure for doing the update, I modify the response data. I've included this for readers who have not yet seen Python's version of the *ternary operator*.

⓫ The `@app.listener` decorators are hooks provided by Sanic to give you a place to add extra actions during the startup and shutdown sequence. This one, `before_server_start`, is invoked before the API server is started up. This seems like a good place to initialize our database connection.

⓬ Use the `Database` helper to create a connection to our PostgreSQL instance. The DB we're connecting to is `restaurant`.

⓭ Obtain a connection pool to our database.

⓮ Use our model (for the `patron` table) to create the table if it's missing.

⓯ Use our model to create a dedicated_listener for database events, listening on the channel `chan_patron`. The callback function for these events is `model.db_event()`, which I'll go through in the next listing. The callback will be called every time the database updates the channel.

⓰ `after_server_stop` is the hook for tasks that must happen during shutdown. Here we disconnect from the database.

---

⑰ This `add_route()` call sends `POST` requests for the `/patron` URL to the `new_patron()` coroutine function.

⑱ This `add_route()` call sends *all* requests for the `/patron/<id:int>` URL to the `PatronAPI` class-based view. The method names in that class determine which one is called: a `GET` HTTP request will call the `PatronAPI.get()` method, and so on.

The preceding code contains all the HTTP handling for our server, as well as startup and shutdown tasks like setting up a connection pool to the database and, crucially, setting up a `db-event` listener on the `chan_patron` channel on the DB server.

Example 4-24 presents the model for the `patron` table in the database.

Example 4-24. DB model for the "patron" table

```python
# model.py
import logging
from json import loads, dumps
from triggers import (
    create_notify_trigger, add_table_triggers)    ❶
from boltons.cacheutils import LRU    ❷

logger = logging.getLogger('perf')

CREATE_TABLE = ('CREATE TABLE IF NOT EXISTS patron('    ❸
                'id serial PRIMARY KEY, name text, '
                'fav_dish text)')
INSERT = ('INSERT INTO patron(name, fav_dish) '
          'VALUES ($1, $2) RETURNING id')
SELECT = 'SELECT * FROM patron WHERE id = $1'
UPDATE = 'UPDATE patron SET name=$1, fav_dish=$2 WHERE id=$3'
DELETE = 'DELETE FROM patron WHERE id=$1'
EXISTS = "SELECT to_regclass('patron')"

CACHE = LRU(max_size=65536)    ❹

async def add_patron(conn, data: dict) -> int:    ❺
    return await conn.fetchval(
        INSERT, data['name'], data['fav_dish'])

async def update_patron(conn, id: int, data: dict) -> bool:
    result = await conn.execute(    ❻
        UPDATE, data['name'], data['fav_dish'], id)
    return result == 'UPDATE 1'

async def delete_patron(conn, id: int):    ❼
    result = await conn.execute(DELETE, id)
    return result == 'DELETE 1'
```

```
async def get_patron(conn, id: int) -> dict:  ❽
    if id not in CACHE:
        logger.info(f'id={id} Cache miss')
        record = await conn.fetchrow(SELECT, id)  ❾
        CACHE[id] = record and dict(record.items())
    return CACHE[id]

def db_event(conn, pid, channel, payload):  ❿
    event = loads(payload)  ⓫
    logger.info('Got DB event:\n' + dumps(event, indent=4))
    id = event['id']
    if event['type'] == 'INSERT':
        CACHE[id] = event['data']
    elif event['type'] == 'UPDATE':
        CACHE[id] = event['data']['new']  ⓬
    elif event['type'] == 'DELETE':
        CACHE[id] = None

async def create_table_if_missing(conn):  ⓭
    if not await conn.fetchval(EXISTS):
        await conn.fetchval(CREATE_TABLE)
        await create_notify_trigger(
            conn, channel='chan_patron')
        await add_table_triggers(
            conn, table='patron')
```

❶ You have to add triggers to the database in order to get notifications when data changes. I've created these handy helpers to create the trigger function itself (with `create_notify_trigger`) and to add the trigger to a specific table (with `add_table_triggers`). The SQL required to do this is somewhat out of scope for this book, but it's still crucial to understanding how this case study works. I've included the annotated code for these triggers in Appendix B.

❷ The third-party `boltons` package provides a bunch of useful tools, not the least of which is the `LRU` cache, a more versatile option than the `@lru_cache` decorator in the `functools` standard library module.[3]

❸ This block of text holds all the SQL for the standard CRUD operations. Note that I'm using native PostgreSQL syntax for the parameters: $1, $2, and so on. There is nothing novel here, and it won't be discussed further.

❹ Create the cache for this app instance.

---

3 Obtain boltons with `pip install boltons`.

❺ I called this function from the Sanic module inside the `new_patron()` endpoint for adding new patrons. Inside the function, I use the `fetchval()` method to insert new data. Why `fetchval()` and not `execute()`? Because `fetchval()` returns the primary key of the new inserted record![4]

❻ Update an existing record. When this succeeds, PostgreSQL will return `UPDATE 1`, so I use that as a check to verify that the update succeeded.

❼ Deletion is very similar to updating.

❽ This is the read operation. This is the only part of our CRUD interface that cares about the cache. Think about that for a second: we don't update the cache when doing an insert, update, or delete. This is because we rely on the async notification from the database (via the installed triggers) to update the cache if any data is changed.

❾ Of course, we do still want to use the cache after the first `GET`.

❿ The `db_event()` function is the callback that `asyncpg` will make when there are events on our DB notification channel, `chan_patron`. This specific parameter list is required by `asyncpg`. `conn` is the connection on which the event was sent, `pid` is the process ID of the PostgreSQL instance that sent the event, `channel` is the name of the channel (which in this case will be `chan_patron`), and the payload is the data being sent on the channel.

⓫ Deserialize the JSON data to a dict.

⓬ The cache population is generally quite straightforward, but note that update events contain both new and old data, so we need to make sure to cache the new data only.

⓭ This is a small utility function I've made to easily re-create a table if it's missing. This is really useful if you need to do this frequently—such as when writing the code samples for this book!

This is also where the database notification triggers are created and added to our `patron` table. See Example B-1 for annotated listing of these functions.

That brings us to the end of this case study. We've seen how Sanic makes it very simple to create an API server, and we've seen how to use `asyncpg` for performing queries

---

4 You *also* need the `RETURNING id` part of the SQL, though!

via a connection pool, and how to use PostgreSQL's async notification features to receive callbacks over a dedicated, long-lived database connection.

Many people prefer to use object-relational mappers to work with databases, and in this area, SQLAlchemy (*https://www.sqlalchemy.org*) is the leader. There is growing support for using SQLAlchemy together with asyncpg in third-party libraries like asyncpgsa (*https://oreil.ly/TAKwC*) and GINO (*https://oreil.ly/a4qOR*). Another popular ORM, Peewee (*https://oreil.ly/pl0Gn*), is given support for asyncio through the aiopeewee (*https://oreil.ly/76dzO*) package.

Other Libraries and Resources

There are many other libraries for asyncio not covered in this book. To find out more, you can check out the aio-libs project (*https://oreil.ly/40Uf_*), which manages nearly 40 libraries, and the Awesome asyncio project (*https://oreil.ly/SsC_0*), which bookmarks many other projects compatible with the asyncio module.

One library that bears special mention is aiofiles (*https://oreil.ly/6ThkG*). As you may recall from our earlier discussions, I said that to achieve high concurrency in Asyncio, it is vitally important that the loop never block. In this context, our focus on blocking operations has been exclusively network-based I/O, but it turns out that disk access is also a blocking operation that will impact your performance at very high concurrency levels. The solution to this is aiofiles, which provides a convenient wrapper for performing disk access in a thread. This works because Python releases the GIL during file operations so your main thread (running the asyncio loop) is unaffected.

The most important domain for Asyncio is going to be network programming. For this reason, it's not a bad idea to learn a little about socket programming, and even after all these years, Gordon McMillan's "Socket Programming HOWTO" (*http://bit.ly/2sQt2d6*), included with the standard Python documentation, is one of the best introductions you'll find.

I learned Asyncio from a wide variety of sources, many of which have already been mentioned in earlier sections. Everyone learns differently, so it's worth exploring different types of learning materials. Here are a few others that I found useful:

- Robert Smallshire's "Get to Grips with Asyncio in Python 3" talk (*https://oreil.ly/S5jRX*), presented at NDC London in January 2017. This is by far the best YouTube video on Asyncio I've come across. The talk may be somewhat advanced for a beginner, but it really does give a clear description of how Asyncio is designed.

- Nikolay Novik's "Building Apps with Asyncio" slides (*https://oreil.ly/ufpft*), presented at PyCon UA 2016. The information is dense, but a lot of practical experience is captured in these slides.

- Endless sessions in the Python REPL, trying things out and "seeing what happens."

I encourage you to continue learning, and if a concept doesn't stick, keep looking for new sources until you find an explanation that works for you.

## CHAPTER 5

Concluding Thoughts

When substantial new features appear in Python, they're new for everybody. I have nearly two decades' experience with Python, but I still found Asyncio difficult to learn—even taking into account that I had already worked with Twisted and Tornado on previous projects, so event-based programming was not new to me. I found the asyncio API to be much more complex than I had expected. Part of this was due to a lack of high-level documentation.

Now, having spent the time to learn how to use Asyncio in Python, I feel a lot more comfortable with it, and this progression will likely be similar for you too. There is a coherent structure and purpose behind the design of the API, and hopefully this book will make it much easier for you to learn than it was for me. With a basic understanding in place, I'm now finding it quite easy to write new Asyncio-based code without having to constantly refer back to the docs: this is a very good sign, and certainly isn't the case with all the standard library modules.

There are still some rough edges, though. The asyncio standard library will continue to have a large, fine-grained API, since it caters to both framework designers and end-user developers. This means that we—as end-user developers—will have to learn which parts of the API are applicable to us and which are not. In time, as the third-party library ecosystem for asyncio grows and matures, we will likely find ourselves working with those library APIs rather than the raw asyncio standard library API. Existing libraries like aiohttp and Sanic are good examples of this. The asyncio API itself will also continue to improve as more people gain experience with it.

I also made unexpected discoveries along the way: by happy coincidence, it turned out that I needed to finally learn ZeroMQ at around the same time this book was being written, and I'm finding that asyncio in combination with pyzmq makes network programming a joy. My recommendation for the best way to learn Asyncio is to experiment, try things out and have fun.

A Short History of Async Support in Python

Despite having been part of the Python standard library for a long time, the asyncore module suffers from fundamental flaws following from an inflexible API that does not stand up to the expectations of a modern asynchronous networking module.

Moreover, its approach is too simplistic to provide developers with all the tools they need in order to fully exploit the potential of asynchronous networking.

The most popular solution right now used in production involves the use of third-party libraries. These often provide satisfactory solutions, but there is a lack of compatibility between these libraries, which tends to make codebases very tightly coupled to the library they use.

—Laurens van Houtven, PEP 3153 (May 2011): Asynchronous IO Support (*https://oreil.ly/pNyro*)

The goal of this appendix is to describe a little of the history behind async programming in Python, and the point I want to make—which still amazes me when I think about it—is that the key innovation that we've been awaiting for 20 years was *language syntax.*

Many people will be surprised by this, but Asyncio is *not* the first attempt that has been made to add support for asynchronous network programming to Python, as is discussed next.

In the Beginning, There Was asyncore

[Compared to asyncore,] Twisted is better in pretty much every possible way. It's more portable, more featureful, simpler, more scalable, better maintained, better documented, and it can make a delicious omelette. Asyncore is, for all intents and purposes, obsolete.

—Glyph ca. 2010 on Stack Overflow (*https://oreil.ly/4pEeJ*)

asyncore should really be considered a historical artifact and never actually used.

—Jean-Paul Calderone ca. 2013 on Stack Overflow (*https://oreil.ly/oWGEZ*)

Support for so-called *asynchronous features* was added to Python a long time ago, in the `asyncore` module. As you can tell from the preceding quotes, reception of `asyncore` was lukewarm, and usage low. What is jaw-dropping, to this author at least, is *when* this module was added: in Python 1.5.2! This is what it says at the top of *Lib/asyncore.py* in the CPython source:

```
# -*- Mode: Python -*-
#   Id: asyncore.py,v 2.51 2000/09/07 22:29:26 rushing Exp
#   Author: Sam Rushing <rushing@nightmare.com>

# ===============================================================
# Copyright 1996 by Sam Rushing
```

Furthermore, the first paragraph of the Python documentation for `asyncore` (*https://oreil.ly/tPp8_*) says the following, which could easily appear in *today's* documentation for `asyncio`:

> This module provides the basic infrastructure for writing asynchronous socket service clients and servers.
>
> There are only two ways to have a program on a single processor do "more than one thing at a time." Multithreaded programming is the simplest and most popular way to do it, but there is another very different technique, that lets you have nearly all the advantages of multithreading, without actually using multiple threads. It's really only practical if your program is largely I/O bound. If your program is processor bound, then preemptive scheduled threads are probably what you really need. Network servers are rarely processor bound, however.

1996, huh? Clearly it was already possible to manage multiple socket events in a single thread in Python back then (and, in fact, much earlier than this in other languages). So what has changed in the past quarter-century that makes Asyncio special now?

The answer is language syntax. We're going to be looking at this more closely in the next section, but before closing out this window into the past, it's worth noting a small detail that appeared in the Python 3.6 docs for `asyncore` (ca. December 2016):

> Source code: Lib/asyncore.py
>
> *Deprecated since version 3.6:* Please use `asyncio` instead.

The Path to Native Coroutines

Recall that I'm using the term *Asyncio* to refer to both the Python language syntax changes, and the new `asyncio` module in the standard library.[1] Let's dig into that distinction a little more.

Today, support for asynchronous programming in Python has three distinct components, and it's interesting to consider when they were added:

Language syntax: generators
> Keyword `yield`, added in Python 2.2 (2001) in PEP 255 (*https://oreil.ly/35Czp*) and enhanced in Python 2.5 (2005) in PEP 342 (*https://oreil.ly/UDWl_*) with the `send()` and `throw()` methods on generator objects, which allowed generators to be used as coroutines for the first time.
>
> Keyword `yield from`, added in Python 3.3 (2009) in PEP 380 (*https://oreil.ly/38jVG*) to make it much easier to work with *nested* yields of generators, particularly in the case where generators are being used as makeshift (i.e., temporary) coroutines.

Language syntax: coroutines
> Keywords `async` and `await`, added in Python 3.5 (2015) in PEP 492 (*https://oreil.ly/XJUmS*), which gave first-class support to coroutines as a language feature in their own right. This also means that generators can again be used as generators, even inside coroutine functions.

Library module: `asyncio`
> Added in Python 3.4 (2012) in PEP 3156 (*https://oreil.ly/QKG4m*), providing batteries-included support for both framework designers and end-user developers to work with coroutines and perform network I/O. Crucially, the design of the event loop in `asyncio` was intended to provide a common base upon which other existing third-party frameworks like Tornado and Twisted could standardize.

These three are quite distinct from each other, although you could be forgiven confusion since the history of the development of these features in Python has been difficult to follow.

The impact of new syntax for `async` and `await` is significant, and it's having an effect on other programming languages too, like JavaScript, C#, Scala, Kotlin, and Dart.

It took a long time and a lot of thinking by the thousands of programmers involved in the Python project to get us to this point.

---

1 `asyncio` was added in Python 3.4.

Supplementary Material

This appendix contains some additional code related to the case studies presented in the book. You might find this material helpful to round out your understanding of the examples.

Cutlery Example Using Asyncio

"Case Study: Robots and Cutlery" on page 14 analyzed a race condition bug caused by multiple threads modifying the cutlery records in the global "kitchen" object instance. For completeness, here is how we might create an async version of the solution.

There is a specific point I want to highlight about the *observability* of concurrency in the asyncio approach, shown in Example B-1.

Example B-1. Cutlery management using asyncio

```
import asyncio

class CoroBot():  ❶
  def __init__(self):
    self.cutlery = Cutlery(knives=0, forks=0)
    self.tasks = asyncio.Queue()  ❷

  async def manage_table(self):
    while True:
      task = await self.tasks.get()  ❸
      if task == 'prepare table':
        kitchen.give(to=self.cutlery, knives=4, forks=4)
      elif task == 'clear table':
        self.cutlery.give(to=kitchen, knives=4, forks=4)
      elif task == 'shutdown':
```

```
        return

from attr import attrs, attrib

@attrs
class Cutlery:
    knives = attrib(default=0)
    forks = attrib(default=0)

    def give(self, to: 'Cutlery', knives=0, forks=0):
        self.change(-knives, -forks)
        to.change(knives, forks)

    def change(self, knives, forks):
            self.knives += knives
            self.forks += forks

kitchen = Cutlery(knives=100, forks=100)
bots = [CoroBot() for i in range(10)]

import sys
for b in bots:
    for i in range(int(sys.argv[1])):
        b.tasks.put_nowait('prepare table')
        b.tasks.put_nowait('clear table')
    b.tasks.put_nowait('shutdown')

print('Kitchen inventory before service:', kitchen)

loop = asyncio.get_event_loop()
tasks = []
for b in bots:
    t = loop.create_task(b.manage_table())
    tasks.append(t)

task_group = asyncio.gather(*tasks)
loop.run_until_complete(task_group)
print('Kitchen inventory after service:', kitchen)
```

❶ Instead of a ThreadBot, we now have a CoroBot. This code sample uses only one thread, and that thread will be managing all 10 separate CoroBot object instances—one for each table in the restaurant.

❷ Instead of queue.Queue, we're using the asyncio-enabled queue.

❸ This is the main point: the only places at which execution can switch between different CoroBot instances is where the await keyword appears. It is *not possible* to have a context switch during the rest of this function, and this is why there is no race condition during the modification of the kitchen cutlery inventory.

The presence of `await` keywords makes context switches *observable*. This makes it significantly easier to reason about any potential race conditions in concurrent applications. This version of the code always passes the test, no matter how many tasks are assigned:

```
$ python cutlery_test_corobot.py 100000
Kitchen inventory before service: Cutlery(knives=100, forks=100)
Kitchen inventory after service: Cutlery(knives=100, forks=100)
```

This really isn't impressive at all: it's an entirely predictable outcome based on the fact that there are clearly no race conditions in the code. And that is *exactly* the point.

Supplementary Material for News Website Scraper

This *index.html* file shown in Example B-2 is required to run the code in "Case Study: Scraping the News" on page 93.

Example B-2. The index.html file required for the web scraping case study

```html
<!DOCTYPE html>
<html lang="en">
<head>
    <meta charset="UTF-8">
    <title>The News</title>
    <style>
        .wrapper {
            display: grid;
            grid-template-columns: 300px 300px 300px;
            grid-gap: 10px;
            width: 920px;
            margin: 0 auto;
        }

        .box {
            border-radius: 40px;
            padding: 20px;
            border: 1px solid slategray;
        }

        .cnn {
            background-color: #cef;
        }

        .aljazeera {
            background-color: #fea;
        }

        h1 {
            text-align: center;
            font-size: 60pt;
```

```
        }
        a {
            color: black;
            text-decoration: none;
        }
        span {
            text-align: center;
            font-size: 15pt;
            color: black;
        }
    </style>
</head>
<body>
<h1>The News</h1>
<div class="wrapper">
    $body
</div>
</body>
</html>
```

It's a very basic template with rudimentary styling.

Supplementary Material for the ZeroMQ Case Study

In "Case Study: Application Performance Monitoring" on page 102, I mentioned that you'll need the HTML file being served to show the metrics charts. That file, *charts.html*, is presented in Example B-3. You should obtain a URL for *smoothie.min.js* from Smoothie Charts (*http://smoothiecharts.org*) or one of the CDNs, and use that URL as the src attribute instead.

Example B-3. charts.html

```
<!DOCTYPE html>
<html lang="en">
<head>
    <meta charset="UTF-8">
    <title>Server Performance</title>
    <script src="smoothie.min.js"></script>
    <script type="text/javascript">
        function createTimeline() {
            var cpu = {};   ❶
            var mem = {};

            var chart_props = {
                responsive: true,
                enableDpiScaling: false,
                millisPerPixel:100,
                grid: {
                    millisPerLine: 4000,
```

```
                fillStyle: '#ffffff',
                strokeStyle: 'rgba(0,0,0,0.08)',
                verticalSections: 10
            },
            labels:{fillStyle:'#000000',fontSize:18},
            timestampFormatter:SmoothieChart.timeFormatter,
            maxValue: 100,
            minValue: 0
        };

        var cpu_chart = new SmoothieChart(chart_props);   ❷
        var mem_chart = new SmoothieChart(chart_props);

        function add_timeseries(obj, chart, color) {   ❸
            obj[color] = new TimeSeries();
            chart.addTimeSeries(obj[color], {
                strokeStyle: color,
                lineWidth: 4
            })
        }

        var evtSource = new EventSource("/feed");   ❹
        evtSource.onmessage = function(e) {
            var obj = JSON.parse(e.data);   ❺
            if (!(obj.color in cpu)) {
                add_timeseries(cpu, cpu_chart, obj.color);
            }
            if (!(obj.color in mem)) {
                add_timeseries(mem, mem_chart, obj.color);
            }
            cpu[obj.color].append(
                Date.parse(obj.timestamp), obj.cpu);   ❻
            mem[obj.color].append(
                Date.parse(obj.timestamp), obj.mem);
        };

        cpu_chart.streamTo(
            document.getElementById("cpu_chart"), 1000
        );
        mem_chart.streamTo(
            document.getElementById("mem_chart"), 1000
        );
    }
    </script>
    <style>
        h1 {
            text-align: center;
            font-family: sans-serif;
        }
    </style>
</head>
<body onload="createTimeline()">
```

```
<h1>CPU (%)</h1>
<canvas id="cpu_chart" style="width:100%; height:300px">
</canvas>
<hr>
<h1>Memory usage (MB)</h1>
<canvas id="mem_chart" style="width:100%; height:300px">
</canvas>
```

❶ cpu and mem are each a mapping of a color to a TimeSeries() instance.

❷ One chart instance is created for CPU, and one for memory usage.

❸ We create a TimeSeries() instance *inside* the onmessage event of the EventSource() instance. This means that any new data coming in (e.g., on a different color name) will automatically get a new time series created for it. The add_timeseries() function creates the TimeSeries() instance and adds to the given chart instance.

❹ Create a new EventSource() instance on the */feed* URL. The browser will connect to this endpoint on our server, (*metric_server.py*). Note that the browser will automatically try to reconnect if the connection is lost. Server-sent events are often overlooked, but in many situations their simplicity makes them preferable to WebSockets.

❺ The onmessage event will fire every time the server sends data. Here the data is parsed as JSON.

❻ Recall that the cpu identifier is a mapping of a color to a TimeSeries() instance. Here, we obtain that time series and append data to it. We also obtain the timestamp and parse it to get the correct format required by the chart.

Database Trigger Handling for the asyncpg Case Study

In "Case Study: Cache Invalidation" on page 115, one of the required Python source files was omitted in the interest of saving space. That file is presented in Example B-4.

Example B-4. triggers.py

```
# triggers.py
from asyncpg.connection import Connection  ❶

async def create_notify_trigger(  ❷
        conn: Connection,
        trigger_name: str = 'table_update_notify',
        channel: str = 'table_change') -> None:
    await conn.execute(
```

```python
        'CREATE EXTENSION IF NOT EXISTS hstore')  ❸
    await conn.execute(
        SQL_CREATE_TRIGGER.format(
            trigger_name=trigger_name,
            channel=channel))  ❹


async def add_table_triggers(  ❺
        conn: Connection,
        table: str,
        trigger_name: str = 'table_update_notify',
        schema: str = 'public') -> None:
    templates = (SQL_TABLE_INSERT, SQL_TABLE_UPDATE,
                 SQL_TABLE_DELETE)  ❻
    for template in templates:
        await conn.execute(
            template.format(
                table=table,
                trigger_name=trigger_name,
                schema=schema))  ❼


SQL_CREATE_TRIGGER = """\
CREATE OR REPLACE FUNCTION {trigger_name}()
  RETURNS trigger AS $$
DECLARE
  id integer; -- or uuid
  data json;
BEGIN
  data = json 'null';
  IF TG_OP = 'INSERT' THEN
    id = NEW.id;
    data = row_to_json(NEW);
  ELSIF TG_OP = 'UPDATE' THEN
    id = NEW.id;
    data = json_build_object(
      'old', row_to_json(OLD),
      'new', row_to_json(NEW),
      'diff', hstore_to_json(hstore(NEW) - hstore(OLD))
    );
  ELSE
    id = OLD.id;
    data = row_to_json(OLD);
  END IF;
  PERFORM
    pg_notify(
      '{channel}',
      json_build_object(
        'table', TG_TABLE_NAME,
        'id', id,
        'type', TG_OP,
        'data', data
      )::text
    );
```

```
    RETURN NEW;
END;
$$ LANGUAGE plpgsql;
""" ❽

SQL_TABLE_UPDATE = """\
DROP TRIGGER IF EXISTS
  {table}_notify_update ON {schema}.{table};
CREATE TRIGGER {table}_notify_update
  AFTER UPDATE ON {schema}.{table}
    FOR EACH ROW
      EXECUTE PROCEDURE {trigger_name}();
""" ❾

SQL_TABLE_INSERT = """\
DROP TRIGGER IF EXISTS
  {table}_notify_insert ON {schema}.{table};
CREATE TRIGGER {table}_notify_insert
  AFTER INSERT ON {schema}.{table}
    FOR EACH ROW
      EXECUTE PROCEDURE {trigger_name}();
"""

SQL_TABLE_DELETE = """\
DROP TRIGGER IF EXISTS
  {table}_notify_delete ON {schema}.{table};
CREATE TRIGGER {table}_notify_delete
  AFTER DELETE ON {schema}.{table}
    FOR EACH ROW
      EXECUTE PROCEDURE {trigger_name}();
"""
```

❶ These functions require asyncpg, although this import is used only to allow Connection to be used in type annotations.

❷ The create_notify_trigger() coroutine function will create the trigger function itself in the database. The trigger function will contain the name of the channel that updates will be sent to. The code for the function itself is in the SQL_CREATE_TRIGGER identifier, and it is set up as a format string.

❸ Recall from the case study example that update notifications included a "diff" section in which the difference between old and new data was shown. We use the hstore feature of PostgreSQL to calculate that diff. It provides something close to the semantics of sets. The hstore extension is not enabled by default, so we enable it here.

❹ The desired trigger name and channel are substituted into the template and then executed.

❺ The second function, `add_table_triggers()`, connects the trigger function to table events like insert, update, and delete.

❻ There are three format strings for each of the three methods.

❼ The desired variables are substituted into the templates and then executed.

❽ This SQL code took me a lot longer than expected to get exactly right! This PostgreSQL procedure is called for insert, update, and delete events; the way to know which is to check the `TG_OP` variable. If the operation is `INSERT`, then `NEW` will be defined (and `OLD` will *not* be defined). For `DELETE`, `OLD` will be defined but not `NEW`. For `UPDATE`, both are defined, which allows us to calculate the diff. We also make use of PostgreSQL's built-in support for JSON with the `row_to_json()` and `hstore_to_json()` functions: these mean that our callback handler will receive valid JSON.

Finally, the call to the `pg_notify()` function is what actually sends the event. *All subscribers* on {`channel`} will receive the notification.

❾ This is standard trigger code: it sets up a trigger to call a specific procedure {`trig ger_name`}() when a specific event occurs, like an `INSERT` or an `UPDATE`.

There are sure to be many useful applications that can be built around notifications received from PostgreSQL.

Supplementary Material for the Sanic Example: aelapsed and aprofiler

The Sanic case study (see *asyncpg* case study) included utility decorators for printing out elapsed time taken by a function. These are shown in Example B-5.

Example B-5. perf.py

```
# perf.py
import logging
from time import perf_counter
from inspect import iscoroutinefunction

logger = logging.getLogger('perf')

def aelapsed(corofn, caption=''):    ❶
    async def wrapper(*args, **kwargs):
        t0 = perf_counter()
        result = await corofn(*args, **kwargs)
        delta = (perf_counter() - t0) * 1e3
```

```
        logger.info(
            f'{caption} Elapsed: {delta:.2f} ms')
        return result
    return wrapper

def aprofiler(cls, bases, members):  ❷
    for k, v in members.items():
        if iscoroutinefunction(v):
            members[k] = aelapsed(v, k)
    return type.__new__(type, cls, bases, members)
```

❶ The aelapsed() decorator will record the time taken to execute the wrapped coroutine.

❷ The aprofiler() metaclass will make sure that every member of the class that is a coroutine function will get wrapped in the aelapsed() decorator.

Index

About the Author

Caleb Hattingh first came across Python at version 1.5.2, learned the basics from printouts of Andrew Kuchling's online PDF notes, and started working with it seriously around 2001, shortly after the release of Python 2.0. It was an interesting time: Caleb's main tools were MATLAB and Delphi, modems in South Africa still made loud noises, Java was at 1.3, C# 1.0 had not yet shipped, and YouTube would not exist for another four years. In Python, Caleb saw a flexible tool that could be wielded to fit any problem.

Testing that hypothesis, Caleb has since applied Python to a wide variety of domains including chemical data modeling, hotel bookings and CRM software, websites, financial management software, chemical reactor modeling, coal combustion dynamic simulation, online learn-to-code training software, GPS tracking software, and most recently software-defined networking.

Similarly discontiguous are the themes in Caleb's publications: this book, *Using Asyncio in Python*, is his third work for O'Reilly, with previous titles being *Learning Cython* (*https://oreil.ly/7v4le*) (video) and *20 Python Libraries You Aren't Using (But Should)* (*https://oreil.ly/3m2iq*). The common theme for Caleb, if any, seems to be finding complex concepts and trying to teach them. Caleb can be found at *https://github.com/cjrh*.

Colophon

The animal on the cover of *Using Asyncio in Python* is a frog of the genus *Hyla*. *Hyla* belongs to the tree frog family Hylidae and consists of 17 living species of frog in Europe, northern Africa, and Asia.

Most of these species are small frogs under 2 inches in length. Their hind legs are longer than their forelegs, and the digits of the hands and feet end in adhesive discs. Depending on the species, as well as temperature, humidity, and mood, skin color ranges from bright to olive green, gray, brown, and yellow. Males have a vocal sac that amplifies their mating calls. These frogs live in forest habitats and breed in lakes, ponds, and swamps. They typically eat arthropods.

All species of *Hyla* are considered common; however, they are all potentially threatened by habitat loss and degradation. Many of the animals on O'Reilly covers are endangered; all of them are important to the world.

The cover illustration is by Karen Montgomery, based on a black-and-white engraving from *English Cyclopedia*. The cover fonts are Gilroy Semibold and Guardian Sans. The text font is Adobe Minion Pro; the heading font is Adobe Myriad Condensed; and the code font is Dalton Maag's Ubuntu Mono.

O'REILLY®

There's much more where this came from.

Experience books, videos, live online training courses, and more from O'Reilly and our 200+ partners—all in one place.

Learn more at oreilly.com/online-learning